D0212920

Into the Breach

_____

Into the Breach

SAMUEL BECKETT AND THE
ENDS OF LITERATURE

Thomas Trezise

PRINCETON UNIVERSITY PRESS
PRINCETON, NEW JERSEY

Copyright © 1990 by Princeton University Press
Published by Princeton University Press, 41 William Street,
Princeton, New Jersey 08540
In the United Kingdom: Princeton University Press, Oxford

All Rights Reserved

Library of Congress Cataloging-in-Publication Data

Trezise, Thomas, 1953–
Into the breach : Samuel Beckett and the ends of
literature / Thomas Trezise.
Includes index.
1. Beckett, Samuel, 1906–   —Fictional works.
2. Beckett, Samuel, 1906–   Molloy. 3. Beckett, Samuel,
1906–   Malone meurt. 4. Beckett, Samuel, 1906–
Innommable. I. Title.
PQ2603.E378Z89   1990   843'.914—dc20   90-8557

ISBN 0-691-06789-9 (acid-free paper)

Publication of this book has been aided by a grant from the
Paul Mellon Fund of Princeton University Press

This book has been composed in Linotron Baskerville

Princeton University Press books are printed on acid-free paper
and meet the guidelines for permanence and durability of the
Committee on Production Guidelines for Book Longevity of the
Council on Library Resources

Printed in the United States of America by Princeton University Press,
Princeton, New Jersey

3   5   7   9   10   8   6   4   2

*For Susan
and for my parents*

———————————

CONTENTS

PREFACE

THE READING presented here focuses almost exclusively on Samuel Beckett's trilogy of novels and on the conception of subjectivity articulated therein. Its purpose is twofold: on the one hand, to place Beckett within a configuration of thinkers whose understanding of subjectivity remains incompatible with the totalizing claims of phenomenology, and on the other, to challenge in so doing the assumptions underlying virtually the entire corpus of Beckett criticism. Regarding this second objective, it is not my intention to conduct a sustained polemic against any particular critic or group of critics but rather, through a critique of its foundation, to place in question the ideology that grew out of phenomenology in the forties and fifties and has since pervaded the interpretation of Beckett's work. I refer of course to existential humanism. There may well be no writer of this century who has more radically questioned the foundations of humanism than Samuel Beckett—and no writer who has spawned a corporation of critics more determined to ignore the consequences of that questioning. This determination frequently surfaces as the professed belief that, in the end, Beckett restores human dignity through his humor—as though the tenor of that humor were self-evident and not in the least subversive. Or else it is claimed, no less frequently and unreflectively, that the ultimate horizon of a text supposedly centered on the despair of the human condition remains the redemptive value of art itself. At any rate, the various ways in which Beckett's fundamentally critical work has been recuperated all rely on an unexamined notion of the human subject. Indeed, this is why most of the criticism devoted to his work amounts to an exercise in ideology rather than in genuine reflection; and this is why one can only begin to read Samuel Beckett by questioning that notion as thoroughly as he himself does.

It will therefore come as no surprise if this study resembles to some extent a prolegomenon. Not only must the interpretation of Beckettian subjectivity start from scratch, but the essentially comparative or intertextual nature of this interpretation precludes even the pretense of an "exhaustive" study devoted exclusively to Beckett's work. I am all the less inclined to apologize for this as the trilogy foregrounds its own intertextuality (thus placing in question the very possibility of its totalization), and as Beckett's stature as a thinker fully reveals itself only when his work is seen in relation to that of other major contemporary figures. The first objective mentioned above, namely, this very comparison of Beckett with such thinkers as Freud, Bataille, Blanchot, and Derrida, emerges from their common, if in some cases entirely implicit, rejection of phenomenology. That the "failure" of phenomenology is here articulated in phenomenological terms is not incongruous with a text whose central preoccupation is the necessity of naming that which both conditions and exceeds denomination.

I would like to thank all those who have helped me during the various stages of my work. The theoretical inspiration for the book originated in a seminar conducted at Yale University by Joseph Libertson. Fredric Jameson, Peter Brooks, Peter Bien, and Denis Hollier have all provided helpful criticism and vital encouragement. More recently, my friend and colleague, Alain Toumayan, read the manuscript in its entirety, offering commentary that has contributed significantly to the improvement of the text and for which I am deeply grateful. The interest and support of my colleagues at Princeton, especially Victor Brombert, Lionel Gossman, Suzanne Nash, and François Rigolot, have helped to sustain my commitment to the project. Its realization was facilitated by the generous initiative of Suzanne Nash, the patience, savoir-faire, and enthusiasm of my editor, Robert Brown, and the expert copyediting of Paula Wissing.

The book would never have materialized without the unfailing support of my parents, and without the sympathy, wit, and intelligence of my wife, Susan Brison.

Princeton and New York
December 1989

Into the Breach

Introduction

THE BREACH

To be an artist is to fail.
—Beckett

BETWEEN 1946 and 1951, Samuel Beckett composed the novel *Mercier et Camier* and the short story "Premier amour," both withheld from publication until 1970; the play *Eleuthéria*, which remains unpublished to this day, as well as the play that first earned him widespread public recognition, *En attendant Godot*; the stories and texts later collected in *Nouvelles et textes pour rien*; and the so-called trilogy of novels (*Molloy*, *Malone meurt*, *L'Innommable*), which he would subsequently call "toute mon oeuvre"[1] and on which the present study will focus.[2] What seems initially

[1] Quoted in Pierre Mélèse, *Samuel Beckett* (Paris: Seghers, 1966), 136. The sentence in its entirety reads as follows: "J'écrivis toute mon oeuvre très rapidement, de 1946 à 1950." While this may appear to suggest that what Beckett calls his "oeuvre" would include some if not all of the other works written between 1946 and 1950, it is clear from a further reference to the "oeuvre" that the latter specifically denotes the trilogy: "A la fin de mon oeuvre, il n'y a rien que poussière: le nommable. Dans le dernier livre, *L'Innommable*, il y a complète désintégration. Pas de *Je*, pas de *Avoir*, pas de *Etre*, pas de nominatif, pas d'accusatif, pas de verbe. Il n'y a pas moyen de continuer. La toute dernière chose que j'ai écrite, *Textes pour rien*, a été une tentative pour sortir de cette attitude de désintégration, mais ce fut un échec" (137). There is some disagreement concerning the date at which Beckett actually completed the *Textes pour rien*, which were begun in 1950 and published in 1955. On the basis of available evidence, however, it seems safe to assume that the greater portion of this work was finished by 1951 at the latest.

[2] For an exhaustive source of information concerning the composition of all but the most recent of Beckett's works, see Richard L. Admussen, *The Samuel Beckett Manuscripts: A Study* (Boston: G. K. Hall, 1979).

most remarkable about this period, which encompasses the legendary "siege in the room,"[3] is of course the sheer volume of work produced by a writer otherwise known for his extreme reticence. Yet it was also during these years that Beckett began to write in French, only later translating his works into English,[4] and that, in his prose, he abandoned third- in favor of first-person narration.[5] This adoption of the first person bespoke, from "Premier amour," "La Fin," "L'Expulsé," and "Le Calmant" to the trilogy and the thirteen *Textes pour rien*, an extraordinary intensification of Beckett's concern with the problem of subjectivity, and furthermore, came at the very moment

[3] See especially Deirdre Bair, *Samuel Beckett: A Biography* (New York: Harcourt, 1978), chap. 15.

[4] In subsequent years, there will be a number of exceptions to this rule, virtually all of which involve dramatic rather than prose texts. In most cases, the translation from English to French is Beckett's own. The substantive questions raised by Beckett's self-translation have only recently begun to receive sustained scholarly attention. I shall not attempt to evaluate the initial results of this research here.

[5] It is true that in *Watt*, written during the Second World War and published in 1953, as well as in *Mercier et Camier*, the third-person narrator temporarily assumes the mode of the first person. In *Mercier et Camier*, this conversion lasts all of a sentence (the first one): "Le voyage de Mercier et Camier, je peux le raconter si je veux, car j'étais avec eux tout le temps" (*Mercier et Camier* [Paris: Minuit, 1970; Minuit 10/18, 1972], 7). The strategic motivation of such a device, which may be understood as the need to remedy the most glaring fallacy of third-person narration by providing it with an explicit epistemological foundation, is no less evident in *Watt*, whose narrator explains: "And so always, when the impossibility of my knowing, of Watt's having known, what I know, what Watt knew, seems absolute, and insurmountable, and undeniable, and uncoercible, it could be shown that I know, because Watt told me, and that Watt knew, because someone told him, or because he found out for himself" (*Watt* [Paris: Olympia Press, 1953; New York: Grove Press, 1981], 127–28). While the intervention of the first person is much more extensive and interesting in *Watt* than in *Mercier et Camier*, its ostensible function is still to insure rather than to question the authority of the narrator. As for his late prose, from *Comment c'est* (1961) to *Stirrings Still* (1988), it can easily be argued that Beckett's use of the various pronominal modes (including that of the second person) is entirely informed by the reorientation to which I allude here.

when French intellectual life experienced the overwhelming influence of existential phenomenology, especially in its Sartrian tendency. While the historical coincidence of these two developments may not have fostered a distinct phenomenological school of Beckett criticism,[6] it certainly favored the pervasive association of Beckett's work with the ideology of existential humanism. And since this ideology derives from a phenomenological understanding of the human subject, any interpretation taking issue with it must ask the basic and long-neglected question whether his explicit preoccupation with the status of the subject necessarily makes of Beckett a phenomenologist, and hence whether his mature prose genuinely lends itself to a phenomenological reading. The present study was born of this question, or more precisely, of the conviction that the phenomenological approach gains whatever insight it may afford from a conspicuous blindness to the dimension of Beckett's prose that signals the exhaustion or failure of phenomenology itself, and that reflects moreover his fundamental affinity with such relatively marginal but important figures as Georges Bataille and Maurice Blanchot, and, a generation later, the more publicized philosophers of difference, Gilles Deleuze and Jacques Derrida.[7] What

---

[6] See, however, Wolfgang Iser, "Subjektivität als Selbstaufhebung ihrer Manifestationen. S. Beckett: *Molloy, Malone Dies, The Unnamable*" and "Ist das Ende hintergehbar? Fiktion bei Beckett," in *Der implizite Leser* (Munich: Fink, 1972), 252–75 and 391–413. Iser's readings exhibit an awareness of the philosophically paradoxical nature of Beckett's work but remain determined by an orthodoxy grounded in subjectivity as consciousness, negation, or *Selbstaufhebung*. A more reductive and less convincing attempt to develop a phenomenological interpretation of Beckett is to be found in David Hesla, *The Shape of Chaos: An Interpretation of the Art of Samuel Beckett* (Minneapolis: University of Minnesota Press, 1971). It will become clear that, from the point of view of this study, nothing is more questionable than a statement such as the following: "The reflexive structure of consciousness as laid out by Sartre is . . . the philosophical 'model' or 'type' of the interpretation of the self to which Beckett comes in the later works, and especially in the third volume of the trilogy" (ibid., 190).

[7] Although I wish here to underscore a general affinity, I would also

unites these thinkers, in their very diversity and in the different relation of each to Nietzsche, Freud, and Heidegger, is the sustained interest in a "general economy"[8] that remains strictly irreducible to the universe of phenomenology. In Beckett's own case, this interest emerges in its most condensed form from a short text on painting entitled "Three Dialogues," which, with the possible exception of *Proust*, comes closer than any other of his publications

---

refer the reader to Bataille, "La Vérité dont nous sommes malades," and Blanchot, "Le Vide et l'appel de l'oeuvre," in *Les Critiques de notre temps et Beckett*, ed. Dominique Nores (Paris: Garnier, 1971), 42–51 and 118–25. Bataille's article was originally published as "Le Silence de Molloy" in *Critique* 48 (1951) and Blanchot's as " 'Où maintenant? Qui maintenant?' " in the *Nouvelle Revue Française* 10 (1953). Blanchot's was later reissued in *Le Livre à venir* (Paris: Gallimard, 1959), where it occupies the strategic center of the section entitled "Où va la littérature?" English translations of Bataille's and Blanchot's essays can be found in *Samuel Beckett: The Critical Heritage*, ed. Lawrence Graver and Raymond Federman (London: Routledge, 1979), 55–64 and 116–21. The most pertinent text by Deleuze is undoubtedly *Différence et répétition*. Those by Derrida which I would cite in this context are *La Voix et le phénomène, L'Ecriture et la différence, De la grammatologie*, and *Marges*.

⁸ The term is Bataille's. See especially *La Part maudite*, précédé de *La Notion de dépense* (Paris: Minuit, 1967), 23–80. When Bataille remarks: "Passer des perspectives de l'économie *restreinte* à celles de l'économie *générale* réalise en vérité un changement copernicien: la mise à l'envers de la pensée" (64), he alludes to a form of thought whose principle is not negation or what I shall call separation ("l'économie *restreinte*") but communication or difference. ("General" is not understood by Bataille as the mere contrary of "particular" and is not to be confused with a term such as "collective." For Bataille, the collective is simply a generalization of the particular, whereas the general economy corresponds to the impersonal perspective of an alterity irreducible to any particular or general identity.) Among the many predicates of subjectivity in the general economy that attest to the affinity between Bataille and Beckett, this study will emphasize 1) im-possibility or powerlessness, in its correlation to what will variously be called a compulsion, an exigency, a force, an imperative, a necessity, or an obligation; 2) dispossession (Bataillian *dépense* or *perte*); 3) *non-savoir* or error. See also Derrida, "De l'économie restreinte à l'économie générale, un hégélianisme sans réserve," *L'Ecriture et la différence* (Paris: Seuil, 1967; Seuil, Points, 1979), 369–407, and the brilliant explication of the general economy in Joseph Libertson, *Proximity: Lévinas, Blanchot, Bataille and Communication* (The Hague: Nijhoff, 1982), 9–55.

to the statement of an artistic credo. As the text dates from 1949, it may also be read as a highly suggestive preface to the trilogy itself.

Beckett begins by denouncing the assumption in painting that "the domain of the maker is the domain of the feasible."[9] Asked by his bemused interlocutor what other domain there can be for the maker or artist, he replies: "Logically none. Yet I speak of an art turning from it in disgust, weary of its puny exploits, weary of pretending to be able, of being able, of doing a little better the same old thing, of going a little further along a dreary road" (*TD* 17). Although the "dreary road" here describes no less than the whole of Western painting from da Vinci to Masson,[10] Beckett's characteristically irreverent criticism assumes an even broader pertinence to the extent that it associates the predicate of feasibility with a certain understanding of artistic *expression* in general:

> Among those whom we call great artists, I can think of none whose concern was not predominantly with his expressive possibilities, those of his vehicle, those of humanity. . . . The much to express, the little to express, the ability to express much, the ability to express little, merge in the common anxiety to express as much as possible, or as truly as possible, or as finely as possible, to the best of one's ability. (*TD* 19)

At issue, then, is the understanding of expression *as* feasibility, as "ability," as "possibility" or power. The assump-

---

[9] Samuel Beckett and Georges Duthuit, "Three Dialogues," in *Samuel Beckett: A Collection of Critical Essays*, ed. Martin Esslin (Englewood Cliffs, N.J.: Prentice-Hall, 1965), 19. Reprinted from *Transition forty-nine* 5 (1949). All further references will be to the reprint and will be given in the text after the initials *TD*. As readers of Beckett well know, "Three Dialogues" is a very stylized text that could even lend itself to performance. In Samuel Beckett, *Disjecta*, ed. Ruby Cohn (New York: Grove Press, 1984), the editor states that "Beckett alone wrote the dialogues that 'merely reflect, very freely, the many conversations we [Beckett and Duthuit] had at that time about painters and painting' " (14).

[10] I refer to this text exclusively for the study of Beckett himself and do not intend to evaluate his remarks on painting.

tion that Beckett initially denounces, to the effect that the domain of the maker is the domain of the feasible, may therefore be restated as the assumption that the domain of expression is the domain of the possible, that expression itself is power. For our purposes, the question then becomes whether, or rather in what way, expression *as* power assumes a specific concept of subjectivity, and whether the nature of this same concept might not shed some additional light on what Duthuit petulantly dismisses as "a violently extreme and personal point of view" (*TD* 17).

It is here in fact that the use of the term "expression" reveals its predominantly strategic value. For while expression, manifestation, and representation all embody a single concept of subjectivity, the first may be said to indicate most immediately the ground of that concept. The "ex-" of "ex-pression" clearly denotes, in other words, an exteriority or outside the originary separation from which constitutes the interiority of the subject or the subject *as* interiority. From Descartes to Husserl and Sartre, subjectivity has indeed been conceived precisely as this separation from exteriority, as Blanchot will observe in his remarkable and remarkably condensed critique of the "I am":

> "I am" (in the world) tends to mean that I am, only if I can separate myself from being: we deny being—or, to illustrate this by a particular case, we deny, we transform nature— and, in this negation which is work and which is time, beings accomplish themselves and men stand erect in the freedom of the "I am." What makes me myself is this decision to be as separated from being, to be *without* being, to be that which owes nothing to being, which takes its power from the refusal to be, the absolutely "denatured," the absolutely separate, that is, the absolutely absolute.[11]

Subjectivity as separation or negation founds a "feasible" world—a world of work or action, of dialectical temporalization, of decision, of freedom, and of power. These last,

[11] Maurice Blanchot, *L'Espace littéraire* (Paris: Gallimard, 1955; Gallimard, Folio Essais, 1988), 337–38.

essentially synonymous predicates recall in particular the Sartrian for-itself, whose ceaselessly championed freedom *is* its power *not* to be, to be only as the nothingness, the negation of .or separation from being. As such, and entirely in accordance with the philosophical tradition from which it is descended, the for-itself represents the very interval in being in which being appears to subjectivity, and so accounts for the phenomenal exteriority of being itself, that is, for being itself *as* phenomenal exteriority. Its freedom and power characterize a universe whose unconditioned term, whose origin or "absolute" remains negation or separation, a universe in which therefore the separation *from* exteriority precedes, founds, and conditions any and every relation *to* exteriority.

Given this definition of the concept of subjectivity in which expression is presumably grounded, one must ask what relation there can be between expression and power. Since, as Blanchot remarks, power *is* separation, it seems paradoxically that power can be predicated of expression only to the extent that this, like any other relation to exteriority, remains essentially a separation from exteriority, only to the extent that ex-pression itself is foreclosed or suspended. Having grasped or perhaps, in the fashion of Molloy and company, sooner stumbled upon this paradox, which, as Derrida has observed, "is in fact only the phenomenological project in its essence,"[12] Beckett will maintain that "all that should concern us is the acute and increasing anxiety of the relation itself, as though shadowed more and more darkly by a sense of invalidity, of inadequacy, of existence at the expense of all that it excludes, all that it blinds to" (*TD* 21). Regarding the occasional topic of "Three Dialogues," he further remarks:

> The history of painting . . . is the history of its attempts to escape from this sense of failure, by means of more authen-

---

[12] Jacques Derrida, *La Voix et le phénomène* (Paris: PUF, 1967), 23; *Speech and Phenomena*, trans. David B. Allison (Evanston, Ill.: Northwestern University Press, 1973), 22.

tic, more ample, less exclusive relations between representer and representee, in a kind of tropism towards a light as to the nature of which the best opinions continue to vary, and with a kind of Pythagorean terror, as though the irrationality of pi were an offence against the deity, not to mention his creature. (*TD* 21)

Thus, for Beckett, the history of painting is the history of an art whose attempts to escape from a sense of failure, "by means of more authentic, more ample, less exclusive relations between representer and representee," are themselves both produced and exceeded by that very sense of failure. Relation as separation and the power it entails appear, in other words, to be conditioned by a larger economy of which they themselves are not predicates. By denouncing the assumption that "the domain of the maker is the domain of the feasible," by insisting that "all that should concern us is the acute and increasing anxiety of the relation itself," Beckett demands of art that it interrogate, rather than simply assume, its own possibility. To do so will not mean to dismiss the concept of expression in favor of another, but to focus above all on the apparently untenable association of expression and power. As our subject is Beckett himself, however, and not Masson or van Velde, it will further be necessary to approach the problem of expression strictly with respect to the writer's own "vehicle," namely, language.

Taking as its clue the very way in which Beckett formulates this problem—by dissociating expression and power and, at least implicitly, language and the phenomenological understanding of subjectivity—the following section on Derrida's critique of the Husserlian theory of signification seeks to develop the problem more fully than does Beckett's own highly epigrammatic text. My extended discussion is motivated by the capacity of this critique to help clarify the general implications of "Three Dialogues" as well as by the heuristic role it plays throughout the subsequent reading of the trilogy.

Expression *as* power remains problematic to the extent, again, that power itself means separation, and hence can be said to characterize a relation to exteriority such as that which expression presumably denotes only if the latter is foreclosed or suspended. As Derrida notes regarding the theory of language in Husserl's *Logische Untersuchungen*: "By a strange paradox, meaning [*vouloir-dire*] would isolate the concentrated purity of its *ex-pressiveness* only at the moment when the relation to a certain *outside* is suspended."[13] Derrida will point out that *vouloir-dire* not only means meaning but designates as well the power of expression, a *dire* governed entirely by a *vouloir* (*VP* 36–39/33–37). The two senses of the term in fact imply each other; for although, unlike Frege, Husserl does not distinguish between sense (*Sinn*) and meaning (*Bedeutung*),[14] it is clear that, for him, meaning refers exclusively to a sense intended by consciousness and which remains fully accessible only within the province of the latter's *vouloir* or power, that is, only if the relation to a certain outside is suspended. Accordingly, and as the title of Derrida's second chapter ("The Reduction of Indication") suggests, the nature and status of expression (*Ausdruck*) will fully emerge

[13] Derrida, *La Voix et le phénomène*, 22; *Speech and Phenomena*, 22. This work will hereafter be cited in the text as *VP*, followed by page references to the French original; page references to the English translation, which has frequently been modified, are given after a slash. Derrida's critique bears for the most part on the first of Husserl's *Logische Untersuchungen*.

[14] See Edmund Husserl, *Logische Untersuchungen*, 6th ed. (Tübingen: Niemeyer, 1980), vol. 2, pt. 1, 52–53; *Logical Investigations*, trans. J. N. Findlay (New York: Humanities, 1970), 1:292. Having first defined these terms as synonymous, Husserl later distinguishes between them in his *Ideen zu einer reinen Phänomenologie und phänomenologischen Philosophie*, vol. 3, bk. 1 of the *Husserliana* (The Hague: Nijhoff, 1950), 304; *Ideas: General Introduction to Pure Phenomenology*, trans. W. R. Boyce Gibson (New York: Collier, 1962), 319. The wider sense ascribed to *Sinn* in this text constitutes in itself a commentary on the difficulties encountered in the *Investigations*.

only on the basis of a preliminary reduction of indication (*Anzeichen*), or more precisely, of the "entanglement" (*Verflechtung, enchevêtrement*) of indication and expression. This reduction entails essentially the suspension of all communication, "both because expression [in real colloquy] indicates a content forever hidden from intuition, that is, the lived experience of others, and because the ideal content of the *Bedeutung* and the spirituality of expression are therein united to sensibility" (*VP* 22/22).[15] In communication, in other words, expression remains entangled with or contaminated by indication because its content ("the lived experience of others") is not immediately present to intuition and—which amounts to the same—because it requires the mediation of irreducibly sensible signs (whether phonic or graphic). In short, expression is indicative and hence other than or outside of itself as long as it comprises a relation to exteriority or alterity. Expression in the Husserlian sense of the term, purified of all indication, can be grasped only "in a language without communication, in speech as monologue, in the completely muted voice of 'solitary mental life' (*im einsamen Seelenleben*)" (*VP* 22/22), in the silent soliloquy of the subject.

The reduction of indication, which will presumably afford access to the purity of expression, nevertheless suspends the relation to a *certain* outside, "only to a certain outside, for this reduction will not efface but rather reveal, within pure expressiveness, the relation to an object, the intending [*visée*] of an objective ideality, which stands face to face with the meaning-intention, the *Bedeutungsintention*" (*VP* 22–23/22). If *de facto* the relation to exteriority

---

[15] Derrida's text reads as follows: "(à la fois parce que l'expression y indique un contenu à tout jamais dérobé à l'intuition, à savoir le vécu d'autrui, et parce que le contenu idéal de la *Bedeutung* et la face spirituelle de l'expression s'y unissent à la face sensible)." It is clear that "le vécu d'autrui" is the expressive content hidden from intuition and not that from which such content is hidden; I have therefore corrected the English translation, which reads "from the lived experience of another."

remains forever indicative, *de jure* it is expressive. The reduction of indication makes it possible to describe the *essence* of this relation. Expression itself involves a relation to
exteriority, but this relation and this exteriority or objective ideality remain *within* consciousness. The distinction
between indication and expression may accordingly be
said to correspond to the distinction between two kinds of
"exteriority," as well as to a host of others that structure
Husserl's text, including the distinction between fact and
right, existence and essence, reality and ideality, and between the sensible and the spiritual or phenomenological
voice.[16] Derrida will essentially focus, neither on one nor
on the other term of any of these distinctions, but on distinction or separation itself. He will ask whether the Husserlian distinction between expression and indication, as
between two radically heterogeneous types of sign, and
those which correspond to it, are not themselves conditioned by the structure of the sign in general—and this
with all due precaution, since the question of the sign in
general, of the essence of the sign, appeals as it were despite itself to the very distinctions it is destined to interrogate.[17]

How then does one distinguish the expressive from the
indicative sign? And whence the privilege of the phenomenological voice? We have observed that indication entails
or rather *is* the mediation of irreducibly sensible signs.
Since, however, it is of the nature of the sensible world that
one occurrence of the same sign may very well differ from
another, a sign can be recognized *as the same* only by virtue
of the abstraction or reduction of this difference, that is,
of the sensible world itself. This reduction yields conversely a same that is necessarily ideal:

> A signifier (in general) must be formally recognizable in spite
> of, and through, the diversity of empirical characteristics
> that may modify it. It must remain the *same* and be able to

[16] See below, n. 18.
[17] See Derrida's own discussion of this question, *VP* 23–27/23–26.

be repeated as such despite and across the deformations to which the empirical event necessarily subjects it. A phoneme or grapheme is necessarily always different, to some extent, each time that it is presented in an operation or a perception, but it can function as a sign and in general as language only if a formal identity enables it to be reissued and recognized. This identity is necessarily ideal. (*VP* 55–56/50)

It is this identity or sameness that distinguishes the expressive from the indicative sign. And since the sameness of the expressive sign is necessarily ideal, it is irreducible to any and all of its occurrences within the real or sensible world:

Insofar as the unity of the word . . . is not to be confused with the multiplicity of sensible events entailed by its use nor taken to depend on it, the *sameness* of the word is ideal, it is the ideal possibility of repetition and it loses nothing through the reduction of *any* or *all* empirical events marked by its appearance. (*VP* 45/41)

The purported reducibility of the sensible or indicative confers upon the spiritual or expressive an independence such that the former may be said, in a certain sense, to derive from the latter as from its origin. Indeed, of the many distinctions already mentioned (inside/outside, expression/indication, sensible/spiritual, *de facto/de jure*, existence/essence, reality/ideality, etc.), each reflects an imbalance intrinsic to the valorization of one term over the other. In each case, moreover, the privileged term assumes the value of originarity, the status of *archē*, precisely because it is already if implicitly understood as *telos*. The commanding or preeminent *telos* of Husserl's theory of the sign will, however, presently become clear. For the moment, it is sufficient to note that the reduction of the sensible evidently applies to that which is other than the spiritual or ideal sameness of the sign, that it applies, in other words, to the *body* of the sign, which, by virtue of its opac-

ity, accounts for the dissimulation of meaning in communication.

This reduction of the body of the sign suspends once
again the relation to a certain outside, which is of course
to say that it suspends as well a certain relation. Not only
this relation, as we have seen, but also this outside may be
qualified as sensible, since it is the body that necessitates
the mediation of irremediably sensible signs in intersubjective or communicative discourse and that explains the in-
accessibility of the other's lived experience to intuition.
The certain outside is therefore to be understood as the
arena in which meaning or *vouloir-dire* suffers loss or alteration. Its reduction yields another outside *within* consciousness and whose structure is sufficiently complex to justify
quoting Derrida at length:

> Ex-pression is exteriorization. It imparts to a certain outside
> a sense which is first found in a certain inside. We suggested
> above that this outside and this inside were absolutely pri-
> mordial: the outside is neither nature, nor the world, nor a
> real exteriority relative to consciousness. We must now be
> more precise. The *bedeuten* intends an outside which is that
> of an ideal ob-ject. This outside is then ex-pressed, goes out
> of itself into another outside which is still "in" consciousness:
> expressive discourse . . . as such and in essence, does not
> need to be effectively uttered in the world. Expressions as
> meaningful signs are thus a twofold going-forth out of itself
> of sense (*Sinn*) in itself, existing in consciousness, in the with-
> oneself or next-to-oneself that Husserl first determined as
> "solitary mental life." (*VP* 34–35/32–33)

In fact, the outside within consciousness is double. It is
first determined as that of an ideal ob-ject (*Gegen-stand*)
whose very ob-jectivity reflects the phenomenal interval in
which the object manifests itself as a function of intentionality. This relation of subject to object is essentially a separation and is granted logical and temporal priority to expression itself. Indeed, just as indication may be said to
derive from expression, so expression appears to derive

from a pre-expressive stratum of sense or meaning. *But not in the same way.* Whereas indication alters an expressive same, expression merely reproduces the same of the pre-expressive. The second outside internal to consciousness is the expressive repetition, re-presentation or reproduction of a same that precedes expression itself. Since the latter alters nothing, however, its derivation from or subordination to the pre-expressive can only be explained by the implicit *telos* which, as I earlier suggested, is also and at once the *archē* of this theory and of phenomenology in general, and which is separation—the ob-jectivity of the object in relation to an intending subject, its presence to consciousness, which is also the presence of consciousness to itself, "the with-oneself or next-to-oneself that Husserl first determined as 'solitary mental life.' " Thus, expression, which *is* the reduction of indication, assumes its privilege precisely because it reproduces and hence preserves separation and that which separation makes possible. In its disembodiment, the expressive signifier reduces the dissimulation of the signified, re-presents it to consciousness and does so immediately, without delay, in the present. In other words, expression involves both a reduction of the extensive or spatial and a simultaneous valorization of the purely temporal, and therefore necessitates, within transcendental consciousness itself, and with the same *telos* in view, a further distinction between speech and writing.[18]

I have observed that the reduction of indication pertains to that which is other than the sameness of the sign, be the sign graphic or phonic. In either case, to be sure, this reduction produces a same; but precisely because it does so of two distinct modes of sensibility, it cannot and does not reduce this distinction. Within the phenomenological reduction, the graphic sign is divested of its empirical exten-

[18] It should be noted that the thematization of the functional difference between expression and indication in terms of speech and writing is fully developed by Derrida rather than Husserl. However, this thematization is clearly suggested at several points in Husserl's text, from which it also provides a useful transition to the trilogy.

sion or spatiality but remains nonetheless spatial in its very ideality:

> The ideal form of a written signifier . . . is not in the world, and the distinction between the grapheme and the empirical body of the corresponding graphic sign separates an inside from an outside, phenomenological consciousness from the world. And this is true of every visible or spatial signifier. Yet every non-phonic signifier involves, within its very "phenomenon," in the phenomenological (nonworldly) sphere of experience where it is given, a spatial reference; the sense of being "outside," "in the world," is an essential component of its phenomenon. (*VP* 85/76)

As with those already cited, moreover, the distinction between the graphic and the phonic sign, between writing and speech, is hierarchized in view of a certain *telos*, the more conspicuously so as, in contrast to the others, it does not correspond to the fundamental distinction between outside and inside but rather is established *within* phenomenological consciousness itself. Writing is devalorized because, by virtue of its own ineliminable visibility, the graphic sign does not lend itself to the immediate re-presentation of the pre-expressive. It thus remains indicative to the extent that, like any sign in communicative or intersubjective discourse, the graphic sign within consciousness is the very dissimulation of that which it purportedly represents. This is not the case with the phonic sign or speech, which, within the phenomenological or transcendental sphere itself, assumes an "apparent transcendence" with respect to writing:

> The "apparent transcendence" of the voice thus results from the fact that the signified, which is always by essence ideal, the "expressed" *Bedeutung*, is immediately present in the act of expression. This immediate presence results from the fact that the phenomenological "body" of the signifier seems to efface itself at the very moment it is produced. It seems already to belong to the element of ideality. It phenomenolog-

> ically reduces itself, transforms into pure diaphaneity the worldly opacity of its body. This effacement of the sensible body and its exteriority is *for consciousness* the very form of the immediate presence of the signified. (*VP* 86/77)

Thus, the phonic sign is privileged inasmuch as it is its own effacement or erasure. The *telos* of Husserl's theory of the sign, in terms of which this privilege is determined and which Derrida defines as presence (the immediate or present presence of the signified to consciousness, which is also and at once the presence of consciousness to itself), may also be understood as the effacement of the sign or of signification in general. The phonic sign alone effects this instantaneous self-effacement, for the phenomenological voice speaks and hears/understands itself (*s'entend*) "in the same instant" (*im selben Augenblick*). The sameness of the instant itself reflects its separation not only from other instants (whence the concept of temporal *ekstasis* and the determination of past and future as modes of the present), but also from the other of temporality so understood, that is, extension or spatiality. The absolute separation of space and time through the instantaneous self-effacement of the sign recalls a classical gesture in the history of philosophy in its valorization of mind, soul, or spirit over body or, in more contemporary and more problematic terms, of consciousness over language.

Now the effacement of the sign in Husserlian phenomenology finds its ostensible justification in the very purposelessness (*Zwecklosigkeit*) of the sign itself. The sign is purposeless, pointless, without finality or *telos* to the extent that it merely re-presents and hence remains exterior and posterior to the originary, pre-expressive presentation of the ideal object to consciousness. Within phenomenological or transcendental consciousness, in other words, the sign as re-presentation (*Vergegenwärtigung*) of an originary presentation (*Gegenwärtigung*) is entirely superfluous: the immediate relation of consciousness to its object necessarily dispenses with the mediation of the sign. And it is on this originary presentation, which is both the *telos* and the *archē*, the *principium*, the very principle of principles of phenomenology, that Derrida's critique of Husserl will focus its greatest energy. As Derrida himself observes: "The instant as point, the identity of experience present to itself in the same instant, thus bears the whole burden of this demonstration" (*VP* 67/60). The question becomes whether the *im selben Augenblick*, as the absolute separation of time and space, indeed whether separation itself and the phenomenological universe it articulates are not themselves conditioned by signification.

The *im selben Augenblick* denotes the simultaneity of a double presence: "the *presence* of sense *both as the object's being before us* open to view and *as proximity to self in interiority*" (*VP* 83/75). Presence is *at once* that of the object to consciousness and that of consciousness to itself; or, according to one of Husserl's more celebrated dicta, "All consciousness is consciousness *of* something," that is, both consciousness of its object and non-thetic or non-positional consciousness of itself. What must be emphasized here is that the separation constitutive of the ob-jectivity of the object, of its presence, *is* phenomenological consciousness. In other words, consciousness is the very form in which the object appears—and does so, through the reduction of its own empirical alterity, always as the same. We have furthermore noted, with respect to the sign, that its sameness is necessarily ideal. Such is the case as well with the pre-expressive object, which emerges only from the reduction of its real or empirical diversity. And as with the sign, it is the very ideality of the ideal object that guarantees the possibility of its being indefinitely repeated or re-presented as the same. This re-presentation does not, however, initially appear to require the mediation of the sign, since it is presumably the return or reactivation of an originary, pre-expressive presentation as such. Yet it is, paradoxically, the very possibility of this re-presentation that makes of presentation itself an impossibility. Indeed, an originary presentation could not return at all unless it originarily

opened upon its own absence. The re-presentation or repetition of an originary same could take place, in other
words, only if this same were originarily other than itself.
What returns in repetition is accordingly not the other *of*
an originary same, or another same; rather, it is in repetition and only in repetition that sameness itself originates.
In brief, the origin of phenomenology is necessarily belated or, as Freud would say, *nachträglich, verspätet*: time
would be frozen at its very source if this source were not
already contaminated, so to speak, if the instant or point
were not already entangled with or inhabited by an outside, if time itself, time "as such," *as presence*, did not already differ from and defer itself. This difference, as Derrida clearly suggests, is not a separation: "Space is 'in' time,
it is time's pure leaving-itself, it is the outside-itself as the
self-relation of time. The exteriority of space, exteriority
as space, does not overtake time, it opens as pure 'outside'
'within' the movement of temporalization" (*VP* 96/86).
Thus, the relation of time and space must be thought in
the absence of terms, since this relation precedes and conditions their separation, that is, their constitution as terms,
as such. The "absolute" separation of time and space is
produced by an economy in which the other is not the
other of the same, but rather the same *as* other in its pre-
originary relation to itself, and which remains irreducible
to the universe whose foundation is the separation of same
and other, namely, the universe of phenomenology itself.

This economy may be predicated of signification to the
extent that the latter both invests and exceeds the separation or distinction of time and space and all those distinctions which correspond to it. Needless to say, this will become clear only if signification is no longer thought within
the system of these distinctions, only if one keeps in mind
that that with respect to which signification appears a mere
supplement is in fact produced by signification itself. I refer once again to the pre-expressive object and to the
problem it raises. This object is presumably given as the
same in an originary presentation, and it is the very ideal-

ity or transcendence of its sameness that allows of its indefinite repetition as such. But since, as we have seen, the
possibility of this repetition is also and at once the impossibility of an originary "as such," since an originary same
can only return as such if it is originarily other than itself,
the pre-expressive object is impossible. It is impossible in
the sense not only that, in its purported sameness, it is the
alteration of a difference, but that, in its purported originarity, it is already a repetition or re-presentation. In
short, the pre-expressive object is impossible to the extent
that it does not precede but rather is produced by signification. And this very impossibility, which pertains to the
origin of phenomenology and its system of distinctions,
clearly suggests that that which conditions and produces
this origin is not to be thought in phenomenological terms.
Signification turns out to be both the possibility and the
impossibility of distinction *in general* considered not only
as the origin or *archē* but also as the end or *telos* of phenomenology: on the one hand, the very possibility of its
repetition implies the differential constitution of distinction itself, and hence the impossibility of its originarity,
and on the other, this same possibility, which, as we have
seen, is necessarily ideal, implies as well that distinction as
such is necessarily deferred *ad infinitum*. Consequently, as
Derrida remarks:

> These "essential distinctions" are caught up in the following
> aporia: *de facto, realiter*, they are never respected, and Hus-
> serl recognizes this. *De jure and idealiter*, they vanish since, as
> distinctions, they live only from the difference between right
> and fact, ideality and reality. Their possibility is their impos-
> sibility. (*VP* 113/101)

As both its possibility and its impossibility, signification is
the aporia of phenomenology itself, the other that both invests and exceeds the distinction between same and other,
inside and outside, ideality and reality, right and fact, essence and existence, the transcendental and the empirical,

the spiritual and the sensible, expression and indication, speech and writing, time and space.

It is for this very reason that the economy of signification necessarily appears, from the point of view of subjectivity as consciousness, that is, from the perspective of modern philosophical orthodoxy, paradoxical. And nothing more clearly illustrates the paradoxical character of signification than the concept of belatedness or supplementarity.[19] As we have seen, the possibility of repetition ascribed to distinction locates the "origin" of distinction in difference. In temporal terms, this means that the *Augenblick*, the instant in its sameness, time in its perennial understanding as presence, emerges from a pre-originary difference that is both the entanglement or involvement of time and space and the deferral or delay of their distinction. Difference does not, however, imply a mere absence of time or atemporality, unless of course one insists on thinking difference in terms of that which it makes possible, unless one appeals to the concept of time *as presence* in order to qualify the absence of presence as the absence of time.[20] Rather, difference does indeed imply a temporality without presence and in which, by virtue of its pre-originary non-self-identity, the instant becomes itself only through and as repetition. Thus, the instant not only sup-

---

[19] Derrida acknowledges the decisive influence of Freud when he observes, in reference to Husserl's *Vorlesungen zur Phänomenologie des inneren Zeitbewußtseins*: "It is no accident that *The Phenomenology of Internal Time-Consciousness* both confirms the dominance of the present and rejects the 'after-event' ['après-coup'] of the becoming conscious of an 'unconscious content,' that is, the structure of temporality implied by all of Freud's texts" (*VP* 70–71/63). See his "Freud et la scène de l'écriture," *L'Ecriture et la différence*, 293–340. It is no accident either that Derrida parted ways with Sartre at this point, among others. In his early philosophical works, Sartre's indebtedness to Husserl entails an oft-repeated and virtually identical rejection of Freud.

[20] See Blanchot, *L'Espace littéraire*, 25–28. Blanchot speaks of an "absence de temps" but is careful to point out that this absence of presence or the present is itself a temporal structure, "le temps de l'absence de temps."

plements or takes the place of its pre-originary incompletion but is, as the origin of "time itself," necessarily belated.
Yet this belatedness or supplementarity pertains, as I have
suggested, to distinction or separation in general and
hence, as Derrida observes, to consciousness or the for-itself:

> What we would ultimately like to suggest is that the for-itself
> of self-presence (*für-sich*) . . . arises within the movement of
> supplementarity as originary substitution, in the form of the
> "in the place of" (*für etwas*), that is, as we have seen, in the
> very operation of signification in general. The *for-itself* would
> be an *in-the-place-of-itself*: put *for itself*, instead of itself. The
> strange structure of the supplement appears here: a possi-
> bility belatedly produces that to which it is said to be added
> on. (*VP* 99/88–89)

In other words, signification belatedly produces the for-
itself, to which it is then (mis)construed as a supplement.
The strange structure of supplementarity fosters what Joseph Libertson has called, in reference to Emmanuel Lévinas's critique of the *cogito*, "an 'unbelievable' involvement
of Effect and Cause":[21] consciousness belatedly manifests
that which produces it and, as effect, becomes the cause of
its own cause. "The *cogito*, in its entirety, is an 'illusion,' "
Libertson remarks, "the illusion that the effect may precede, found and condition its cause"[22]—an illusion, that is,
in terms of the only truth known to the *cogito*, namely, separation.[23] Only an economy of which separation is not a

[21] Libertson, *Proximity*, 36.

[22] Libertson, *Proximity*, 35.

[23] In the interest of terminological clarity, I must note that in Libertson's study, to which my own is considerably indebted, the sense of the
term "separation" will most often differ from the sense in which it is used
here, since Libertson insists on its properly Lévinasian acceptation. Thus,
for example, having quoted most of the passage from Blanchot appearing above (p. 8, above; Libertson, *Proximity*, 46), he affirms soon there-
after: "*True* separation is produced by the approach of the exterior whose
incumbence dismantles the principles of identity's adequate closure" (48,
my emphasis). For Libertson, then—and for Lévinas (see especially *Tota-*

predicate, and in which the instant is always already involved with other instants, can produce the unbelievable or paradoxical reversal of cause and effect, before and after, which *is* the *cogito*. The *cogito* or consciousness is thus a moment within a general economy of signification that exceeds its punctuality.

But if temporality represents the Scylla of phenomenology, intersubjectivity is undoubtedly its Charybdis. The foregoing discussion holds that difference belatedly produces distinction or separation and hence suggests that subjectivity ("solitary mental life") is always already intersubjective or, which here amounts to the same, that expression is always already inhabited, as it were, by indication. In this case, indication would no longer denote the other *of* expression, but the non-self-identity of expression itself. Similarly, intersubjectivity would not denote a relation, grounded in separation, between two or more subjects, but the non-self-coincidence of the subject itself and its involvement with an Other that is not another subject. These two components of a single problematic coincide, appropriately enough, when one considers the expression "I am."

Husserl characterizes the personal pronoun "I" as an essentially "occasional" expression, that is, as one whose meaning necessarily depends on the context in which it is uttered. As Derrida points out through an example borrowed from Husserl, this necessity becomes clear if, in a given statement, one replaces the pronoun "I" with an "objective" expression, one whose meaning remains independent of contextual considerations:

> If, for example, I tried to substitute, for the word *I* as it appears in a statement, what I take to be its objective concep-

---

lité et infini [The Hague: Nijhoff, 1961], 23–94)—"true" separation and what Blanchot calls "essential solitude" (as opposed to solitude or separation "in the world") are essentially synonymous: separation describes, within the general economy, a differential unicity that is not a closure or an identity. In contrast to this, my own use of the term, while recognizing its differential constitution, most often equates separation with closure, identity, or negativity.

tual content ("whatever speaker is designating himself"), I
would end up in absurdities. Instead of "I am pleased," I
would have "Whatever speaker is now designating himself is
pleased." Whenever such a substitution distorts the statement, we have to do with an essentially subjective and occasional expression that functions indicatively. (*VP* 105/94)

The expression "I" functions indicatively, in other words,
insofar as its meaning differs from the ideality or sameness
of meaning (*vouloir-dire*, *Bedeutung*) in general. It is indeed
a matter of no little interest why Husserl should maintain,
on the one hand, that the meaning of the word "I" always
so differs, and on the other, that meaning in its very ideality is always the same. Therein perhaps lies, at any rate,
the hidden necessity of the ultimate reduction from which
expression, in its absolute purity, will presumably emerge.
This reduction consists, in Derrida's words, "of putting out
of play, as 'inessential components' of expression, the acts
of intuitive cognition which 'fulfill' meaning" (*VP* 100/90).
The essence and originality of expression thus derive from
the difference between intention (*vouloir-dire*, *Bedeutungsintention*) and intuition: expression is no less expressive,
no less *sinnvoll* or meaningful in the absence of the intuited
object, that is, in the absence of intuition itself. This seems
all the more surprising, of course, as that which initially
distinguished expression from indication was precisely
(the presence of) intuition. Yet we may say, with Derrida,
that *vouloir-dire* in the sense of sense or meaning in fact
requires the reduction of intuition if the very sameness or
ideality of meaning itself is to be preserved. This is clearly
the case with the personal pronoun "I," whose meaning remains the same only if one reduces the possibility of mod-
ification or absence intrinsic to its object. The expression
"I am" must, according to Husserl's own premises, remain
meaningful even in the absence of the speaking subject:

> When I say to myself "I am," this expression, like any other
> according to Husserl, has the status of speech only if it is
> intelligible in the absence of its object, of intuitive presence—
> here, in the absence of myself. It is moreover in this way that

the *ergo sum* is introduced into the philosophical tradition and that a discourse about the transcendental ego is possible. Whether or not I have a present intuition of myself, "I" expresses something; whether or not I am alive, *I am* "means something." Here also the fulfilling intuition is not an "essential component" of expression. Whether or not *I* functions in solitary speech, with or without the self-presence of the speaking subject, it is *sinnvoll*. (*VP* 106/95)

Whether or not the expression "I am" may be fulfilled by the intuition of its object is beside the point. The point is precisely that meaning functions regardless of this contingency: the expression "I am" does not become meaningless (*sinnlos*) if its "author" is absent, unknown, or dead. It is for this reason that, as Derrida notes, "the ideality of the *Bedeutung* here has by virtue of its structure the value of a testament" (*VP* 107/96)—to which one may add that this, like any testament, is *written*. The absence of intuition constitutive of the ideality or sameness of meaning bespeaks the written character of speech itself, the indicative nature of all expression.

Thus, in order to safeguard the purity of expression, Husserl must reduce that very component which alone distinguishes expression from indication. As Derrida points out (*VP* 109/97-98), this reduction is provisional: intuition is bracketed, but only with a view toward its eventual restoration. Yet this merely confirms the selfsame aporia, for the advent of an intuited object adequate to the expression "I am" would entail at one and the same time the substitution of ideality for reality and hence the absence of any intuiting subject capable of proclaiming: "I am." *For subjectivity*, the ideality of meaning, which Husserl determines as the "living present" (*lebendige Gegenwart*), is death itself. Precisely because meaning is ideal, however, its advent is *in reality* indefinitely deferred. In other words, meaning itself is produced as an indefinite futurity, as a *toujours à venir*, by the difference between reality and ideality, by the difference or deferral of distinction or separation in gen-

eral. The meaning or sense of the expression "I am" is possible only by virtue of a difference whose unique *sens* or
direction is toward the outside already within and which,
for subjectivity, spells the impossibility of meaning its self.
Meaning or *vouloir-dire* as act or intention is fundamentally
neither the one nor the other: the involvement of subjectivity with an outside prior to separation describes its passivity with respect to a movement that exceeds the speaker's initiative. Subjectivity indeed expresses itself, but not
on the basis of the freedom and power that are born of
separation. Subjectivity expresses itself to the extent, and
only to the extent, that it has always already been forced
outside of itself, that it is always already intersubjective.
Expression is therefore to be understood as both a compulsion, a necessity or an obligation and, paradoxically, an
im-possibility, the involvement of subjectivity in a universe
without power. Intersubjectivity denotes a relation not
subsequent but rather prior to separation. It may refer to
the intrication or involvement of two or more subjects, but
as this involvement precedes subjectivity itself in its traditional understanding, intersubjectivity designates what
Blanchot calls "Quelqu'un,"[24] an Other that is not another
subject. Indeed, as we shall see in Beckett's trilogy, the necessity and the impossibility of expression do not allude to
another and a greater power. Someone—no one—makes
the speaker speak.

．　．　．

In conceding that, "logically," there is for the maker or artist no domain other than that of the feasible, Beckett refers exclusively to a universe in which the *logos* is determined as separation and in which, as we have seen, one
may predicate power of expression only to the extent that
expression, like any other relation to exteriority, remains a
separation from exteriority, only if expression is fore-

---

[24] *L'Espace littéraire*, 27–28.

closed or suspended. The result, in keeping with the principle of separation or negation itself, is that power and
its corollary, freedom, necessarily become the freedom
and the power *not* to speak. This is confirmed by the
Husserlian theory of the sign, which preserves subjectivity
as domain or as separation, which safeguards "das einsame Seelenleben," precisely by reducing the sign itself.
Phenomenology would thus, by denying the possibility of
a discourse on the transcendental ego, at once deny its
very own possibility. The aporia or paradox in which phenomenology finds itself (un)grounded leads Derrida to the
decisive discovery that the sign both invests its phenomenological reduction and, as the ineluctable repetition of
this reduction attests, ineluctably escapes it. The phenomenological reduction of the sign assumes the form of a moment, destined indefinitely to repeat itself, at which a fugitive Other belatedly summons the philosophical vigilance
it has always already eluded. This Other is not another
subject, nor therefore is it another freedom or another
power: its investment of and escape from subjectivity are
not predicated upon a power to invest or escape. Rather,
the Other denotes that with which, prior to separation,
subjectivity is passively involved, and whose force or pres-
sure animates a movement exceeding closure or separation itself, a movement that is here called ex-pression. Expression bespeaks the failure of separation, what Libertson
has named "the 'weakness' of the negative,"[25] in brief, a
necessity and an im-possibility, the obligation to speak and
the inability not to do so. To the untenable association of
expression and power, Beckett himself will consequently
prefer "the expression that there is nothing to express,
nothing with which to express, nothing from which to express, no power to express, no desire to express, together
with the obligation to express" (*TD* 17). His concession to
common sense must therefore be granted a certain irony:
the logic of separation, which affirms the power of expres-

[25] *Proximity*, 4.

sion only as it simultaneously forecloses expression itself, remains in its very own terms eminently illogical and merely succeeds in underscoring the irreducibility of the *logos* to separation.

Thus, expression pertains to an economy whose "principle" is not separation or negation but their failure. It remains to be seen, however, in what way expression as failure applies specifically to the artist. In denouncing the assumption that "the domain of the maker is the domain of the feasible," while also conceding that for the maker or artist there is "logically" no other, Beckett clearly suggests that the artist has no domain at all, that art itself is essentially homeless.[26] But this, needless to say, begs interpretation. One may, for example, cite Beckett's dictum: "To be an artist is to fail, *as no other dare fail*" (*TD* 21, my emphasis) in support of the claim that the Beckettian conception of art as failure or impossibility reflects the estrangement of art itself from the world of power or feasibility. This is the sense in which Blanchot reads Hegel's celebrated statement that "art is for us a thing of the past": "Art is no longer able to answer the need for absoluteness. What counts absolutely is henceforth the accomplishment of the world, the seriousness of action and the task of real freedom."[27] Art as failure would prove, from this perspective, to be a failure of art historically determined by the metaphysics of separation originating in Descartes and culminating in Hegel, but whose accomplishment begins in earnest only with the inexorable rise of science and technology during the second half of the nineteenth century.

[26] Both "home" and "domain" are here construed as figures of separation. That the artist has no domain, art no home within the logic of separation thus means simply that the artist has no domain at all, nor art any home.

[27] Maurice Blanchot, *Le Livre à venir* (Paris: Gallimard, 1959; Gallimard, Folio Essais, 1986), 265. Hegel's statement, from the *Vorlesungen über die Ästhetik* (Stuttgart: Reclam, 1971), reads as follows: "In allen diesen Beziehungen ist und bleibt die Kunst nach der Seite ihrer höchsten Bestimmung für uns ein Vergangenes" (50).

Science as separation, that is, as the idealization, the objectification or presentation of being, and technology as its implementation, would essentially require a "reduction" of art in general analogous to the reduction of "writing" in the *Logische Untersuchungen*. In other words, the indicative character of writing as the other of speech, and, by analogy, that of literature and the other arts as the other of philosophy, would appear to render them inessential or supplementary to an era whose *telos* is precisely the (re)presentation of being. Perhaps. Yet the analogy itself would clearly imply that art or literature is no more determined by the philosophy of separation and its realization, literary language no more so by language as *technē*, than is writing by speech. In accordance with the strange structure of supplementarity, what is called "literature," what is ostensibly determined by the world of separation and power as a "mere" supplement, would refer in fact to a general economy that both produces that world (and with it the distinction between philosophy and "mere" literature) and exceeds it.[28] The estrangement of literature from the familiar domain of the feasible would not amount to a distinction, nor therefore would it yield but another domain or another familiarity. Rather, the estrangement of literature would describe literature itself as a strangeness constitutive of all familiarity. Art as failure would not denote a failure of art determined by the world of separation, but rather a failure that inhabits separation itself. How is this so? And what does it mean for the artist?

We have seen how signification belatedly produces the for-itself or *cogito*, to which signification is then construed to be a supplement. The strange structure of signification thus conditions the familiar and illusory world of separa-

---

[28] It must be emphasized that the reversal of this or any distinction reinscribes its devalorized term as the other of the distinction itself. By virtue of what Bataille calls "la mise à l'envers de la pensée," the term "literature" would not designate literature in its conventional sense (any more than "writing" in Derrida signifies marks on a page) but rather the condition of possibility both of philosophy and of literature as its excess.

tion, including the reduction of signification itself, or the distinction between expression and indication, speech and writing. However—and as Derrida observes (*VP* 20/20)—this distinction is more *functional* than *substantial*, which is to say that, in the universe of separation, writing as substance can and in the first place always does function as speech. Only in this way, indeed, can we account for the illusion that a word is "the thing itself." This illusion in its priority is not avoidable, for the simple reason that it *is* the *cogito* or consciousness itself: in a universe whose *principium* is separation, what comes first is precisely the effacement of the sign. The philosophy of separation defines language in general as *technē*,[29] as a tool or implement in the service of representation and whose use or implementation, as in Heidegger's description of *das Zuhandene*,[30] is also and at once its dis-appearance. As a certain reading of Heidegger would further suggest, it is only when, as *technē*, language fails or breaks down, only when it becomes unusable, that it becomes conspicuous as well, that it unites the functional and substantial aspects of writing, only then, in short, that language becomes mere "literature." "Mere" literature is useless, that is, both purposeless (*zwecklos*, without *telos*) and powerless insofar as it draws attention to the sign itself and to its essentially indicative or fictional status. Yet precisely in so doing, literature in its very secondarity belies the priority of that world which originates in the dis-appearance of the sign. Necessarily belated with respect to the *cogito*, literature nevertheless bespeaks the uncanny belatedness of the *cogito* itself with respect to the fundamentally immemorial past of signification. The tardy awakening of consciousness to its own illusory priority describes

---

[29] Beckett refers scornfully to the concept of art determined by language or expression in general as *technē* when he describes the painter Bram van Velde as "the first to admit that to be an artist is to fail, as no other dare fail, that failure is his world and the shrink from it desertion, *art and craft*, good housekeeping, living" (*TD* 21, my emphasis).

[30] See Martin Heidegger, *Sein und Zeit*, 15th ed. (Tübingen: Niemeyer, 1979), section 15.

its pre-originary involvement in an economy of signification that both invests or produces and escapes or exceeds
consciousness itself, and may accordingly be characterized
as that which is at once strangest and most familiar to it.
And just as signification is no mere supplement to, but
rather an otherness constitutive of, consciousness, so literature does not merely supplement but rather *is* philosophy
insofar as philosophy is essentially estranged from itself.
The conception of literature as an estrangement of the familiar world of separation not only stresses its basic affinity
with other instances of an economy irreducible to that of
separation, such as death, desire, dream, and myth, but
also implies that literature or art in general is possible as a
supplement to separation only if separation is always already (un)grounded in its own failure. This failure or expression is the very *Unheimlichkeit*[31] from which the familiar and sedative illusion of home, of domain, of abode, the
illusion of "das einsame Seelenleben" itself, emerges.

Thus, what is proper to literature or to literary language
can only be the dispossession of the proper or of separation itself. For the artist or, in this case, the writer, it is,
according to Beckett, no longer a question of attempting
to escape from failure "by means of more authentic, more
ample, less exclusive relations between representer and
representee," by enlarging "the statement of a compro-
mise" (*TD* 16), no longer a question, in other words, of
merely reproducing a world in which literature has no
stake. The task of the writer is rather to open the question
of literature itself as the dispossession of that world, and
most notably of its foundation, the *cogito* or "first person."

---

[31] The word is used here not only in reference to Freud's essay on "Das
Unheimliche" but, more broadly, to acknowledge his understanding,
"avant la lettre," of the general economy. In this respect, it is no accident
that "Das Unheimliche" and *Jenseits des Lustprinzips* were written during
the same period. While *Unheimlichkeit* clearly assumes here both a temporal and an intersubjective significance, its full semantic force cannot be
measured in the absence of more explicitly spatial considerations. See below, chap. 3.

It is hardly surprising, then, that the publication of "Three Dialogues" coincided with Beckett's abandonment of third- in favor of first-person narration, for the discovery of the impossibility of expression and the adoption of that quintessentially personal voice which expresses itself in the impersonality of writing are clearly of a piece. At no time perhaps has Beckett's work been more untimely than when his so-called despair was (mis)construed as the pathos of an existential humanist, and when the Beckettian "I" was hastily (mis)interpreted as an *exemplum* of the phenomenological for-itself. And at no time did his work more compellingly suggest the affinity with a Bataille or a Blanchot, and more unmistakably anticipate a Deleuze or a Derrida. His uncompromising preoccupation with the question of subjectivity gives one to think subjectivity *as a quest(ion)*, as a *recherche* in the Proustian sense of the term, as a search originating in the immemorial dispossession of subjectivity itself. This dispossession, this involvement with an outside already within is what Deleuze, after Bataille, has called a *fêlure* or breach.[32] And it is into the breach that Samuel Beckett writes.

[32] See, for example, Georges Bataille, *L'Erotisme* (Paris: Minuit, 1957), 104–20 (esp. 116) and Gilles Deleuze, *Différence et répétition* (Paris: PUF, 1968), 116–28. I do not mean to suggest that Bataille's and Deleuze's respective uses of this word constitute an explicit genealogy. On the other hand, it is curious that Bataille does not figure among the many sources cited by Deleuze.

Chapter One

DISPOSSESSION

Les vrais paradis sont les paradis qu'on a perdus.
—Proust

THE PROBLEM of time has suffered a rather ignominious fate in the canon of Beckett criticism because its study, when undertaken at all, has either been confined to a squarely phenomenological perspective or, which is most often the case, remained philosophically uninformed.[1] It is for this reason that the reading here proposed, which will focus on the second part of *Molloy* considered as a temporal paradigm for the trilogy as a whole, begins by reviewing and expanding the concept of supplementarity discussed briefly in the introduction. Although it certainly goes against the grain of a literary criticism that, jealous of its fictitious prerogatives, would disclaim any need of philosophy and in so doing merely persist in the ignorance of its own philosophical presuppositions, this "beginning" ascribes no priority to philosophy. Indeed, if the introduction has served its purpose, it might even go without saying that the following prefatory remarks represent what is properly the postface to a certain reading of *Molloy* and more generally of the entire trilogy. Such a reversal is, to be sure, no less the belated product of supplementarity than philosophy itself—when philosophy is literature.

[1] For one of the few exceptions to this rule, see Ross Chambers, "Beckett, homme des situations limites," *Cahiers de la compagnie Madeleine Renaud–Jean-Louis Barrault* 44 (1963): 37–62. Although I would question the distinction between time and atemporality on which Chambers bases much of his study, he nevertheless comes as close as any critic to an accurate description of Beckettian temporality.

When Derrida, in his critique of Husserl, speaks of "the strange structure of the supplement," according to which "a possibility belatedly produces that to which it is said to be added on,"[2] so that signification, having belatedly produced consciousness or the for-itself, is then misconstrued as posterior to it, he describes the problematic origin of the first person in an economy whose principle is not separation but difference, and which remains irreducibly other than that of the first person itself. This origin proves indeed to be genuinely problematic inasmuch as the strange structure of the supplement involves a reversal of historical time, and with it a fundamental discrepancy between the origin of the for-itself and the for-itself *as origin*, between the genesis of consciousness and its misinterpretation of this genesis. The articulation of this same discrepancy is, moreover, at least threefold.

It is important to note first of all that the for-itself as origin not only reverses but simultaneously inaugurates historical time. This becomes clear if, in simplified yet instructive terms, we observe that, as origin, the for-itself is necessarily the origin of . . . , and that its originarity is no less necessarily conferred upon it by that *of which* it is the origin or the essentially non-originary. To be more precise, we may say that the for-itself as origin *of*, or indeed, *for itself*, can be characterized as originary only to the extent that it originarily differs from its self, and hence can only *become* what it is belatedly, "à retardement," *nachträglich*. Whence, in an essay on Freud, the thinker of *Nachträglichkeit*, Derrida's statement that "it is a non-origin which is originary."[3] What is originary, in other words, is not the origin itself but its delay or deferral; what is originary is not a moment, distinct from and prior to another, but a communication of moments preclusive of priority itself; what is originary, in short, is not separation but difference,

[2] *VP* 99/89.

[3] *L'Ecriture et la différence*, 303; *Writing and Difference*, trans. Alan Bass (Chicago: University of Chicago Press, 1978), 203.

which denotes both the pre-originary non-self-identity of
the for-itself and the deferral or delay of its origin, that is,
of its separation. And since, furthermore, this separation
or sameness is achieved only through and as the belated
repetition of a pre-originary difference, the instant at
which the for-itself supposedly becomes what it is corresponds in fact to the return of a past that *is* the very
deferral of temporal priority. However, precisely because
separation coincides with the birth of consciousness or the
for-itself, this past remains essentially immemorial,[4] an irrecoverable "already," while the for-itself, in its very belatedness, inevitably assumes *for itself* the status of origin.
Thus, at one and the same time or, in Husserl's words, "im
selben Augenblick," the for-itself reverses and inaugurates
historical time.

As this very reversal of historical time, the for-itself bespeaks, in the second place—and in correlation to the "already" or irrecoverable past—an indefinite futurity or *à
venir*. Insofar as it assumes *for itself* the status of origin and
becomes the cause of that cause of which it is the effect,
the for-itself necessarily repeats or reiterates—and does so
as though it entirely preexisted—its own genesis. That it
should thus preexist itself means that the for-itself is essentially not yet, yet to come, *à venir*. The punctual moment

---

[4] It should be stressed that the immemoriality of this past characterizes
a difference and *not* a negativity, and hence that it does not, as in Husserl's and Sartre's phenomenological misreading of Freud, define the unconscious as a mere absence of consciousness. The past of consciousness
is un-conscious or im-memorial to the extent that subjectivity is pre-
originarily non-self-identical and that the advent of its sameness coincides
with the belated (and involuntary) repetition of this non-self-identity. The
immemorial past is *both* that which cannot be remembered, insofar as the
involvement of subjectivity with an outside already within impedes the
separation constitutive of consciousness, *and* that which cannot but be remembered, insofar as the very force of this outside animates the repetition that produces consciousness or memory itself. It is clear that the differential temporality of signification cannot be understood unless such
negative or privative prefixes as the "im-" of "immemorial" or the "un-"
of "unconscious" are understood to designate the very failure of negation
or separation.

at which the for-itself, in its supposed separation or sameness, presumably originates "once and for all," is exceeded
by a movement in which the for-itself appears to be both
cause and effect, beginning and end, *alpha* and *ōmega*, and
perhaps most notably in Sartre, Father and Son[5]—or else
not yet the one nor the other, since the first can become
what it is, again, only by virtue of its pre-originary relation
to that of which it is the origin, only, therefore, by virtue
of its own *à venir*. The *à venir*, the "yet to come" or "not
yet," thus recalls the "already" to the extent that it ascribes
a belatedness or futurity to the origin of the for-itself, or
more precisely, to the for-itself *as origin*, in an economy
where the moment or instant is a duration, a delay, a deferral. It is for this reason that Derrida compares the structure of the *für-sich* to that of the *für etwas*, that is, to the
structure of signification in general: the *für-sich* as origin
for itself essentially differs from itself and may accordingly
be said to signify, to stand for, to take the place of, its self.
"The *for-itself* would be an *in-the-place-of-itself*: put *for itself*,
instead of itself."[6] In this sense, the for-itself would represent the pre-originary difference from which its self, in its
traditional definition as consciousness, self-presence, or
separation, belatedly originates. But again, the very structure that produces the for-itself as separation also and at
once produces the temporal reversal by reason of which
the for-itself so understood misunderstands itself as
originary. Only an economy in which the moment is constitutively involved with other moments can yield the unbelievable reversal or confusion of historical time that is

---

[5] Although this is clearly the case in the early philosophical works, the
most striking and certainly, for Sartre's early thought, the most critical
portrayal of subjectivity as simultaneously Father and Son is to be found
in the later autobiographical text, *Les Mots* (1963). The irony of this text
resides of course in its being a literary denunciation of literature or, more
broadly, a written denunciation of writing; it consists, in other words, of
Sartre's debunking his personal myth of self-creation by repeating the
creative gesture it makes possible.

[6] *VP* 99/89.

the for-itself, and because of which it is as though signification were a "mere" supplement to it, as though the return of the "already" in the "not yet" were merely the repetition of an originary same.

The third and final articulation of this discrepancy, correlative to the "not yet" and the "already," is precisely what
Libertson,[7] after Lévinas, has called the "as though" or
comme si, and which one might also call the conditionality
of the for-itself. The conditionality of the for-itself refers
quite literally to its being conditioned by an economy
whose principle—difference—is not its own and in which,
just as the instant becomes the communication of a past
that was never present and a future that never will be, so
the identity or separation of the for-itself turns out to be
an inextricable involvement with the exterior that both invests and exceeds it. The "as though" of the for-itself thus
describes its essentially latent, inactual, or illusory character within a differential economy, as well as the illusory
character of the "unconditional" originarity of the for-itself understood as separation. In other words, it is the
for-itself as difference that conditions its "unconditional"
separation; it is the pre-originary non-self-identity of the
for-itself, or rather the repetition of this non-self-identity,
that yields the impossible reversal by virtue of which it is
as though the for-itself were an originary same; in brief, it
is the strange structure of signification itself that accounts
for the familiar illusion that signification merely supplements the for-itself.

To summarize, one may say that the for-itself "unites the
'not yet,' the 'already,' and the 'as though,' by virtue of its
communicational excess over both punctuality and actual-
ity,"[8] that is, in the terminology of the present study,[9] over
separation. In so uniting the "not yet," the "already," and
the "as though" as articulations of the strange structure of

[7] *Proximity*, 34–37.
[8] Ibid., 37.
[9] See p. 23 above, n. 23.

supplementarity, the for-itself originates, as I have suggested, only *as* the repetition of a difference, as a repetition in the absence of any origin(al)—which is to say that it
is always already a re-presentation, indeed that the very
foundation of modern philosophy is "merely" a story. Told
in the first person. A story whose truth necessarily relies
on the illusion that the first person may preexist its own
genesis. For as we have seen, it is this reversal of historical
time that inaugurates the illusory priority of beginning to
end intrinsic to historical or narrative time itself. A story,
therefore, that can only tell the truth of this illusion at the
price of its self, that can tell the truth of the "as though"
only if it describes its subject as both an "already" and a
"not yet," if its structure embodies the originary *fêlure* or
breach that *is* subjectivity.

．　．　．

These remarks constitute what I should like to consider an
indispensable prolegomenon to the reading of *Molloy*—indispensable inasmuch as the structure of this work, which
critics are inclined either to ignore altogether or to regard
as no more than a curiosity,[10] derives in fact from a necessity intrinsic to Beckett's meditation of subjectivity in its
fundamental affinity with differential thought in general.
Thus *Molloy*, the "origin" of the trilogy, is *two* stories, the
question of whose relation arises not only from their inclu-
sion within a single volume, and not only from their uncanny similarity, but also and especially from the order in
which they are told. For in the first part, Molloy recounts
how, impelled by an obscure imperative, he set out to visit
his decrepit mother, to whom a rather extended voyage

---

[10] Even Blanchot, perhaps Beckett's most astute critic, does not do justice to this structure, which harbors an essential affinity between the two
writers. See *Le Livre à venir*, especially 287–88. Edith Kern ("Moran-Molloy: The Hero as Author," *Perspective* 11 [Autumn 1959]: 183–93) calls
attention to the matter and offers an interpretation whose principle is
somewhat narrowly aesthetic.

brought him no closer but whom he now very much resembles; while in the second (which is almost exactly equal
in length to the first), a former agent named Jacques
Moran tells of having one day received from his superior
"the order to see about Molloy"[11] and proceeded to em-
bark on a journey during which he not only failed to locate
his quarry but came to resemble him more and more. As
even so brief a summary of the novel's double plot cannot
fail to suggest, it is indeed as though Moran were a
younger Molloy, and Molloy's story a later and, as it were,
yet more impoverished version of Moran's. Further parallels between them appear to bear this out. For example,
both Moran and Molloy receive a visitor, certain of whose
traits would lead one to believe that he is in both cases the
same;[12] however, while Molloy's is otherwise but dimly
portrayed and remains in fact entirely anonymous, Gaber
immediately and fully assumes the status of what we are
accustomed to call a character. Moreover, both narrators
begin with a description of their present situation; nevertheless, whereas Molloy, his quest having ended uncere-
moniously in a ditch, can only wonder how he later came
to occupy the very room (his mother's) that earlier eluded
him, Moran is writing at a desk in his own house, to which
he managed to return with only the meager assistance of a
dilapidated umbrella, and from which, having told his
story, he prepares to depart anew in very much the same

[11] Samuel Beckett, *Three Novels* (New York: Grove Press, 1955; Grove
Press Black Cat, 1965), 92. In order to simplify things, I will henceforth
use in the text the following system of reference when quoting from the
trilogy: first, I will give an abbreviation of the French title (*M* for *Molloy*,
MM for *Malone meurt*, *I* for *L'Innommable*); second—including where, as
in the vast majority of cases, I quote in English—the page number of the
original French edition (*Molloy* [Paris: Minuit, 1951], *Malone meurt* [Paris:
Minuit, 1951], *L'Innommable* [Paris: Minuit, 1953]); and third, after a
slash, the page number of the Black Cat edition. English translations are
Beckett's own, except that *Molloy* was translated by Patrick Bowles in col-
laboration with the author.

[12] The visitor is presumably part of a network, arrives on Sunday, is
always thirsty, etc.

condition as that in which Molloy *began* his search. Finally, the physical deterioration suffered by Molloy and Moran both, but which, as I have noted, remains considerably less advanced in the case of Moran, coincides with an increasing discursiveness or errancy of language and, consequently, with an impoverishment of storytelling itself; and yet, the problem of language appears less acute in the second than in the first part of the novel.

Thus, if we regard the two parts of *Molloy* as different versions of the same story, it is clear that the order in which they are told reverses the chronology of that which they tell. There is, in other words, an evident disjunction between what Gérard Genette has called *le temps de l'histoire* and *le temps du récit*,[13] between the time of the story itself and that of its telling, a disjunction that, furthermore, pertains no less to each part individually than to the relation between them. For again, just as the first part of *Molloy* relates what is chronologically second, and the second first, so in each part taken separately does the narrator begin his story at the end. The question of the relation between the two parts of the novel therefore entails the question of the relation of each part to itself; and both may be stated as the question of the relation between *histoire* and *récit*, in which the *récit* reverses the time intrinsic to the *histoire*.

In accordance with this reversal, I will begin at the end (which is of course also the beginning), that is, with the second part of *Molloy*. Here as in the first part, the narrator begins by referring to his present situation:

> It is midnight. The rain is beating on the windows. I am calm. All is sleeping. Nevertheless I get up and go to my desk. I can't sleep. My lamp sheds a soft and steady light. I have trimmed it. It will last till morning. I hear the eagle-owl. What a terrible battle-cry! Once I listened to it unmoved. My son is sleeping. Let him sleep. The night will come when he too, unable to sleep, will get up and go to his desk. I shall be forgotten.

[13] Gérard Genette, *Figures 3* (Paris: Seuil, 1972), 77.

My report will be long. Perhaps I shall not finish it. My name is Moran, Jacques. That is the name I am known by. I am done for. My son too. All unsuspecting. He must think he's on the threshold of life, of real life. He's right there. His name is Jacques, like mine. This cannot lead to confusion. (*M* 153/92)

If the reader takes no special note of the temporal reversal or prolepsis that inaugurates the telling of Moran's story, it is no doubt because, as Genette remarks, " 'first-person' narrative lends itself better than any other to anticipation," but not precisely, as he further maintains, "by the very fact of its avowedly retrospective character, which authorizes the narrator to allude to the future and in particular to his present situation."[14] It is rather the "impossible" reversal of historical time, by virtue of which the narrator belatedly preexists and repeats his or her own genesis, that simultaneously accounts for the avowedly retrospective character of first-person narrative and "authorizes" the narrator to allude to the future. In fact, this "future" is already past, just as the "past" is yet to come; and what is here called the narrator's "present situation" is no more than the moment at which this past and this future communicate, at which the "already" returns as the "not yet." So indeed do the paragraphs quoted above describe both an end and a beginning, so does the present indicative in that most noteworthy statement: "I am done for," refer the reader to a past that is yet to come, to the repetition of an "already" whose pertinence to Moran's ruin, to his insomnia, and to his writing can only be anticipated. At the same time, however, it is to be noted that this paradoxical anticipation of the past parallels the very movement of signification, which produces the illusory priority of separation or sameness to signification itself. In other words, the temporal reversal by reason of which the first person appears to precede, found, and condition its own past subordinates the

[14] Ibid., 106; *Narrative Discourse*, trans. Jane E. Lewin (Ithaca, N.Y.: Cornell University Press), 67.

repetition of the "already" in the "not yet" to the economy of the same, that is, to the economy of what is proper to the first person. Thus, what "authorizes" the narrator to allude to the future is also what fosters the illusory priority of the proper: the economy in which the first person misinterprets itself as originary is also the economy in which the reader misreads a text as meaning what it says. This misreading, *in its priority*, is not avoidable, since it is produced by the strange structure of signification, whereby what comes first is precisely the effacement or oblivion of signification itself, whereby a first reading proves to be the misreading it is only belatedly. Such is the case with Moran's narrative, whose "impropriété" becomes clear, as we shall see, only at the end, that is, only with the return of the beginning.

It is nevertheless no accident that, in the work of a writer as highly self-conscious as Beckett, the problem of the first person should be consistently thematized in terms of "propriété."[15] Indeed, Moran's retrospective self-portrait presents an entirely convincing prototype of the *petit propriétaire*, for whom to have and to be are no less than synonymous. The commonplace of Beckett criticism according to which *Molloy* represents a parting nod to the traditional novel appears moreover to find some justification in the initial concern to situate Moran in his proper time and place:

[15] I use the French word "propriété" because it encompasses a larger number of meanings derived from the Latin *proprius* and pertinent to Beckett than does any one English term. Its principal meanings in current French usage are (1) property as a right; (2) property as that which is possessed; (3) property as distinctive quality or attribute; (4) appropriateness, suitability, correctness. I extend this semantic field to include properness of sense (which is not here distinguished from literalness). "Propriété" is also related etymologically to "propre" in the sense of "capable" and to "propreté" as "cleanliness" (a notion not irrelevant to the understanding of obscenity, scatological and other, in the trilogy). For a useful but theoretically limited discussion of this question, see Olga Bernal, *Langage et fiction dans le roman de Beckett* (Paris: Gallimard, 1969), 31–55.

I remember the day I received the order to see about Molloy. It was a Sunday in summer. I was sitting in my little garden, in a wicker chair, a black book closed on my knees. It
must have been about eleven o'clock, still too early to go to
church. (*M* 153–54/92)

Ever the proprietor, Moran describes his garden as a
"black mass of fragrant vegetation that was mine and with
which I could do as I pleased and never be gainsaid" (*M*
212/127), a place or space of uncontaminated privacy and
solitude where, he says, "I thought I was hidden from any-
body coming into my grounds" (*M* 155/93). The significance of this supposedly hermetic enclosure for the purpose of characterization, or more broadly of the
topological definition of the self, is further clarified when,
at a later date, seized by what is perhaps his most tenacious
fear, Moran the narrator inquires:

Does this mean I shall one day be banished [expulsé] from
my house, from my garden, lose my trees, my lawns, my
birds of which the least is known to me . . . lose and be banished from the absurd comforts of my home [mon intérieur]
where all is snug and neat and all those things at hand without which I could not bear being a man, where my enemies
cannot reach me, which it was my life's work to build, to
adorn, to perfect, to keep? (*M* 220/132)

Reminiscent of the architectural metaphorics of the *cogito*
in Descartes,[16] Moran's property embodies a certain economy (*oikos*, house + *nomos*, management)[17] whose predicates are ascribed to the self and that is here most clearly

[16] I refer specifically to the figures of foundation and of building, as in
the following statement from the *Discours de la méthode*: "Jamais mon des-
sein ne s'est étendu plus avant que de tâcher à réformer mes propres
pensées, et de bâtir dans un fonds qui est tout à moi" (René Descartes,
Oeuvres philosophiques 1, ed. F. Alquié (Paris: Garnier, 1988), 582.

[17] Beckett speaks of Bram van Velde as "the first to admit that to be an
artist is to fail, as no other dare fail, that failure is his world and the
shrink from it desertion, art and craft, *good housekeeping*, living" (*TD* 21,
my emphasis).

articulated as the separation of an inside from an outside, that is, as the properly spatial economy of a "habitation" (from the Latin *habitus*, past participle of *habere*, to have or possess). As in Descartes, moreover, this separation of inside from outside figures the fundamental separation of time and space whereby time itself takes the form of a mere succession of punctualities, a repetition of the same, in brief, a "habit" (derived, like "habitation," from *habitus*). To Moran's "proper place" may thus be said to correspond a time proper or appropriate to the first person and in which it finds itself, so to speak, temporally *chez soi*: his punctuality ("It must have been about eleven o'clock, still too early to go to church"; "If there was one thing displeased me, at that time, it was being late for the last mass" [*M* 157/94]; "I liked punctuality, all those whom my roof sheltered had to like it too" [*M* 163/98]) and his "day of rest" (*M* 154/93) are entirely consonant, in that this rest not only is itself a habit but reflects more generally the self-coincidence of subjectivity as habit(ation). Most remarkable indeed in this paradisiacal scene, aside from the iconographic "black book," is the sitting position, which Moran will be the last of Beckett's characters to assume[18] and which incorporates the very *assise*, the foundation or *Setzung* of the self at home with itself. "Incorporates," however, just as Moran's *petite propriété* "figures" or "embodies": the expression of the temporality proper to the first person in what are properly spatial metaphors suggests from the outset another economy to which the very "propriété" of separation itself does not pertain. And in this respect, the biblical overtones of the beginning of the story—of the *histoire* as distinguished from the *récit*—are no accident either; for not only will Moran be expelled from his habit(ation) but this expulsion will entail the definitive loss of the sitting position, leaving him at best up-

---

[18] Except for Molloy, who only sits, however, when riding his bicycle, with one foot pedaling and the other propped on the front axle. See also n. 22, below.

right with the aid of his umbrella or crutches, in a carica-
ture of human rectitude, and at worst reducing him to that
embodiment of the Fall which is the horizontal, while be-
stowing upon him the inability to stop moving.

It must however be noted that the story begins in earnest only when Moran's paradise, in which "slipped away,"
he observes, "my last moments of peace and happiness" (*M*
155/93), is disturbed by the untimely intrusion of an other
assuming, we soon learn, the form of a messenger named
Gaber. The order that Gaber conveys to Moran, "the order
to see about Molloy," emanates from their common *patron*,
a certain Youdi who—similar in this respect to Knott[19] as
well as to Godot—is most notable throughout the story for
his absence.[20] That Youdi should have chosen Moran, that

[19] Watt's mysterious master in *Watt* and the prototype, as it were, of
both Youdi and Godot. In this strange, obsessional and fascinating novel,
to which I can only allude here, Knott, who is seen by Watt but once,
obscurely, and who never speaks, is the very absence that allows the *semblance* of a meaningful system or structure—the succession of servants,
for example, of which Watt is only one—to function, just as Godot constitutes the couple Vladimir-Estragon and impels the repetition of the
first in the second act, and as Youdi initiates the series Moran-Molloy-
Malone-the Unnamable (not to mention Malone's and the Unnamable's
various delegates). In each case, although in a different manner and to a
different degree, the status of this transcendental figure is placed in question. In the trilogy and in *Watt*, this *mise en question* eventually leads to a
form of madness.

[20] Critics have hastened to draw attention to the "allegorical" elements
in *Molloy* no less than in *En attendant Godot*. Thus, Youdi would stand for
Jehovah, Gaber for Gabriel (the more convincingly so as he arrives at the
hour of the Angelus), etc. No doubt it would be tempting to pursue this
line of thought, not because it is correct (it is not) but because it raises, by
virtue of her very absence from such a configuration, the question of the
female and specifically of the mother in Beckett's work. In the first part
of the novel, of course, this question is more explicit from the very outset,
where Molloy already occupies his mother's room and defines the beginning of his earlier quest as the moment when "having waked between
eleven o'clock and midday (I heard the angelus, recalling the incarnation,
shortly after) I resolved to go and see my mother" (*M* 22/15). My reading
of the relation between Molloy and his mother (see especially chap. 2,
below) would suggest a close connection between the feminine and what

he should send Gaber on a Sunday and require Moran to leave the same day, that he should further require Moran to take his son with him—all of this indicates that the Molloy affair represents, in Moran's own words, "no ordinary one [un travail sortant de l'ordinaire]" (*M* 161/96). Yet the extra-ordinary nature of the Molloy affair does not elicit from Moran a correspondingly extraordinary effort to prepare for his departure but inexplicably deprives him of those very properties or qualities which have ordinarily made of him a successful agent. Indeed, Moran "wastes" no less than one half of the entire narrative in distraction from the task at hand; and even when he attempts to bring his ordinarily methodical mind to bear upon it, he methodically avoids the essence of the task itself: "My concern at first was only with its immediate vexations and the preparations they demanded of me. The kernel of the affair I continued to shirk. I felt a great confusion coming over me" (*M* 163/98). Thus, he first concerns himself in habitual fashion with the problem of transportation—yet does so without having considered the basis on which it must be solved:

> But if I was in the habit of first settling this delicate question of transport, it was never without having, if not fully sifted, at least taken into account the factors on which it depended. For how can you decide on the way of setting out if you do not first know where you are going, or at least with what purpose you are going there? But in the present case I was tackling the problem of transport with no other preparation than the languid cognizance I had taken of Gaber's report. . . . To try and solve the problem of transport under such conditions was madness. Yet that was what I was doing. I was losing my head already. (*M* 164/98)

---

this study calls intersubjective alterity. At any rate, as we shall see, the misunderstanding of the allegorical as that which "stands for" the proper constitutes, according to the temporality described in this chapter, the inevitable point of departure of its own undoing. See n. 24, below.

As this passage suggests, Moran "loses his head" in a very specific sense: his "madness" consists of reversing the order of things, of pondering the question of the *means* of transport to be employed while disregarding the *end*, the purpose or *telos* in whose terms alone that question can be answered. This madness, which characterizes the whole of his preparation, or rather its failure, is underscored by a remark made close upon his long deferred departure:

> It was then the unheard of sight was to be seen of Moran making ready to go without knowing where he was going, having consulted neither map nor timetable, considered neither itinerary nor halts, heedless of the weather outlook, with only the vaguest notion of the outfit he would need, the time the expedition was likely to take, the money he would require and even the very nature of the work to be done and consequently the means to be employed. (*M* 205–6/124)

The adverb "consequently," which in fact ascribes priority to the *telos* of Moran's mission, also and at once bespeaks the very reversal constitutive of the ordinary world of the *agent*, that is, of the instrumental or utilitarian world of decision, of action, and of power, and without which the mission itself cannot properly begin. It is precisely because, without foreknowledge of the end, Moran is constrained to begin at the beginning, that this beginning proves to be essentially a failure to begin. Like Molloy, Moran might very well say: "I began at the beginning, like an old ballocks . . . " (*M* 8/8). His indecision, his *désoeuvrement* or inaction, his powerlessness are attributable to a reversal of that reversal by virtue of which the end precedes, founds, and conditions the beginning, by virtue of which closure or separation precedes, founds, and conditions its own genesis. The extraordinary nature of the Molloy affair has therefore to do with this reversal, which is also a "reinscription."[21] In short, Gaber's untimely intrusion must be

[21] See p. 30, n. 28. To say that this reversal is a "reinscription" means, as we shall see momentarily, that it (re)introduces a temporality wherein,

seen to disrupt Moran's habit(ation) in such a way as to dispossess the economy proper to the first person.

In this connection, it would do well to recall that Gaber is a messenger, and that his duty consists of transmitting to Moran what is essentially a story. As Moran himself suggests, the "great confusion" that comes over him may be traced to the very incompletion of this originary narrative:

> What was I looking for exactly? It is hard to say. I was looking for what was wanting to make Gaber's statement complete. I felt he must have told me what to do with Molloy once he was found. My particular duties never terminated with the running to earth. That would have been too easy. But I always had to deal with the client in one way or another, according to instructions. (*M* 227/136)

It is in vain that Moran repeatedly returns to this question;[22] and it is in vain that we ask whether he simply fails to recall his instructions in their entirety or Gaber so to impart them in the first place, since it is precisely the incompletion of Gaber's statement that informs Moran's *recherche* and is indeed, for that very reason, "difficile à dire." In other words, this incompletion at once produces Moran's search, insofar as "what was wanting to make Gaber's statement complete" represents the end in whose absence the search itself originates, and dispossesses it, insofar as this search can properly originate only as the search for . . . , only if its end precedes, founds, and conditions its beginning. The reversal of this reversal, to which I alluded above and because of which Moran is constrained as it were to begin at the beginning, must therefore be understood to reverse the priority of separation to difference, of closure to signification, and hence to confound priority itself, that is, to reinscribe it within an economy where end and beginning are confused precisely because closure or

---

unlike historical time, which it dissymmetrically conditions and in which alterity is grounded in identity, the only sameness of the instant results from the repetition of its non-self-identity.

[22] See *M* 229/137, 242/145, 247/148, 263/158.

separation is an *inachèvement,* an incompletion or *ouver-
ture.* Thus does Moran's search originate in an absence
of origin or priority such that the search itself becomes the
repetition, not of an originary same, but of its very incompletion. It is in this sense that "Moran making ready to go
without knowing where he was going" is an "unheard of
sight [chose sans précédent]": the *pourquoi* of his search—
its *archē* as well as its *telos*—assumes the form of a "finality
without end" (*M* 185/111) to the precise extent that this
search is conditioned by an economy of signification without end and therefore also without beginning, in which
closure is both an "already" and a "not yet," a past that was
never present and a future that never will be, and of
which presence or the for-itself as consciousness is not a
predicate—which is to say, furthermore, that the *pourquoi*
of Moran's *recherche* is essentially the *pour-soi* of signification itself. Gaber's arrival represents the insistence,
within the habitual or ordinary world of the first person,
of an economy wherein what comes first is not a person
but the immemorial dispossession of the personal. And in
keeping with the profoundly Proustian inspiration of
Molloy, the disruption of Moran's habit(ation) will recall
this "already," this dispossession which conditions all
"propriété," and with it, paradoxically, the proper name
Molloy.

Indeed, what I have called the extraordinary nature of
the Molloy affair is bound sooner or later to direct our attention to Molloy himself. If, as Moran clearly states, the
pourquoi of this affair remains irreducible to the simple apprehension of Molloy, this may very well mean, conversely,
that Molloy is simply not to be apprehended. In other
words, if the Molloy affair involves Moran in a universe
irreducibly other than that of the first person, this involvement plainly suggests that Molloy himself is not to be
thought primarily as another person. The immemorial dispossession to which I just referred implies in fact that subjectivity is always already intersubjective; and the essential
coincidence of the *pourquoi* of the Molloy affair and the

pour-soi of signification would further indicate that the "not yet" of Moran's pursuit is also and at once the "already" of his involvement with another prior to the separation of same and other:

> Molloy, or Mollose, was no stranger to me. If I had had colleagues, I might have suspected I had spoken of him to them, as of one destined to occupy us, sooner or later. But I had no colleagues and knew nothing of the circumstances in which I had learnt of his existence. Perhaps I had invented him, I mean found him ready made in my head. There is no doubt one sometimes meets with strangers who are not entire strangers, through their having played a part in certain cerebral reels. This had never happened to me, I considered myself immune from such experiences, and even the simple *déjà vu* seemed infinitely beyond my reach. But it was happening to me then, or I was greatly mistaken. (*M* 186/111–12)

So evoked, Molloy lends an unexpected precision to the perplexingly vague order "de m'occuper de Molloy" (*M* 153/92)—as though Molloy had always "occupied" or inhabited Moran as the very latency of Moran's own *à venir*. This appears to be confirmed by Moran's description of Molloy, in which their distinction or separation is called into question and which I quote therefore at length:

> He had very little room. His time too was limited. He hastened incessantly on, as if in despair, towards extremely close objectives. Now, a prisoner, he hurled himself at I know not what narrow confines, and now, hunted, he sought refuge near the centre.
> He panted. He had only to rise up within me for me to be filled with panting.
> Even in open country he seemed to be crashing through jungle. He did not so much walk as charge. In spite of this he advanced but slowly. He swayed, to and fro, like a bear.
> He rolled his head, uttering incomprehensible words.

He was massive and hulking, to the point of misshapen-
ness. And, without being black, of a dark colour.
He was forever on the move. I had never seen him rest.
Occasionally he stopped and glared furiously about him.
This was how he came to me [C'est ainsi qu'il me visitait],
at long intervals. Then I was nothing but uproar, bulk, rage,
suffocation, effort unceasing, frenzied and vain. Just the opposite of myself, in fact. It was a change [Cela me changeait].
(*M* 188–89/113)

Most noteworthy here is indeed the "uproar, bulk, rage,
suffocation, effort unceasing, frenzied and vain," that is,
the extent to which Moran resembles Molloy by reason of
the metamorphosis Molloy's "visits" occasion. One cannot
help but think once again of Moran's statement, "I felt a
great confusion coming over me," which in this context
would describe an intersubjective involvement that dispossesses the separation or distinction of those terms chris-
tened Moran and Molloy. That Molloy should return as
the effect of "involuntary memory" implies that this involvement is more fundamental than consciousness itself
and explains why, in the idle hope that he might one day
locate his quarry, Moran subsequently says of Molloy, who
is Moran's own future, who is born of Moran's metamorphosis and is in this sense his son, that he would "grow to
be . . . like a father to me" (*M* 269/161–62). A father in that
Molloy bespeaks the originarity, not of the first person—
Moran—but of its very non-self-identity or dispossession;
and hence also a son, in that the first person is what it is
only if it "has" an *à venir*, only if it is its own future, the
repetition of this originary dispossession. As both the "already" and the "not yet" of the first person, Molloy does
not represent another person so much as the fundamental
impersonality of the first person itself. Whence the necessity of *two* proper names—Molloy and Moran—which anticipate the Unnamable inasmuch as their confusion describes the dispossession that invests all "propriété." Proust
did not say otherwise: the phrase, "les vrais paradis sont

les paradis qu'on a perdus," does not express the nostalgia for an originary presence but attests to the origin of memory in *oubli*, to the origin of subjectivity in its own immemorial loss or dispossession.

Yet Proust's lesson may be learned in more than one way. As Deleuze has pointed out,[23] the "already" or immemorial past of *A la recherche du temps perdu* finds its essential corollary in the "not yet" of a death instinct expressed in the work of art itself. So it is that the closing pages of *Le Temps retrouvé*, inspired by the hero's belated awakening at the *matinée chez la princesse de Guermantes*, portray the *Recherche* as yet to come and confirm the suggestion that dispossession in its investment of "propriété" entails in fact a repetition, and hence in no way a "recovery," of dispossession itself. The novel already written is not the novel yet to be written, any more than the novel one has yet to read is the novel one has just read—unless, of course, this very sameness be predicated of difference, unless "propriété" be understood as the return of dispossession. But the point is this: the very originarity of dispossession, which makes possible the reversal of historical time constitutive of "propriété," describes as well the *irreversibility* of dispossession itself, and with it the fundamental dissymmetry of time. And its pertinence to Beckett: while the intersubjective dimension of this dissymmetry will be fully developed only in the next chapter, it already suggests why what I have called Moran's involvement with another prior to the separation of same and other resurfaces through the intervention of a third who, *in the story*, assumes the form of another and, so to speak, a greater person. For even though Molloy himself may be said to represent the "already" of an intersubjective relation that precedes subjectivity as separation, this does not appear to account for the experience of the relation itself, that is, for the very *compulsion* to repeat the "already" in the "not yet." As we have just seen, however, this intersubjectivity is described less by

<hr />

[23] Gilles Deleuze, *Différence et répétition* 160, n. 1.

Molloy himself than by his pre-originary confusion with Moran, a confusion whose irreducibility to separation implies that the relation between intersubjectivity and separation is itself dissymmetrical. For the moment, then, we can say that repetition is experienced as both a compulsion and an impossibility insofar as this intersubjective relation *conditions* the world of separation, in which subjectivity is presumably able and free *not* to repeat and in which, as a result, it can explain the fact of its own compulsion and powerlessness only in terms of another and greater power. Thus, the impersonal Other of the separation of same and other is misunderstood as another Same, a third *person*— the forever absent Youdi—who, in the second half of *Molloy*, initiates repetition with an order concerning which Moran notes that "it was impossible for me to refuse" (*M* 158/95), who customarily speaks in the imperative or rather the "prophetic present [futur prophétique]" (*M* 181/109), under whose compulsion Moran will leave his "propriété" or habit(ation), "in accordance with instructions received" (*M* 218/131).

But if the first half of this narrative represents essentially a failure to begin, the second represents no less essentially a failure to end. Ever unable to recall the purpose of his mission, Moran is compelled as it were to defer the mission itself: "But I also told myself . . . that the longer I took to find Molloy the greater my chances of remembering what I was to do with him" (*M* 229–30/138). To the *oubli* of the "already" corresponds the *attente* of a "not yet," a time of increasing indeterminacy and virtually unrelieved monotony during which Moran not only proves so distracted that he fails to profit from the encounter with a figure uncannily reminiscent of Molloy (*M* 242–44/145–47)[24] but is in his very distraction inexorably impelled toward the Molloy he himself has yet to become:

[24] This is not to say that the figure in question is Molloy or that Moran could have acted. The point is rather that this episode indicates the impossibility of action in the universe in which Moran is now engaged.

And on myself too I pored, on me so changed from what I was. And I seemed to see myself ageing as swiftly as a day-fly. But the idea of ageing was not exactly the one which offered itself to me. And what I saw was more like a crumbling, a frenzied collapsing of all that had always protected me from all I was always condemned to be. (*M* 247/148)

The question of Moran's being amounts in fact to the question of his having, for in the pages that follow his departure, the metamorphosis he suffers will take the form of a dispossession in what is, so to speak, the proper sense of the term: Moran will lose those properties which had previously distinguished his person or character, as well as the "possession" of his body,[25] not to mention his truant son, much of his clothing, and most of his money. To be sure, he will, once again upon the unexpected arrival of Gaber and at Youdi's behest, return home, although, like its owner, the home to which he returns bears but a faint resemblance to its former self. Yet it is precisely here, at home and in the end, after nearly a year of fruitless wandering, that Moran underscores the fundamental dispossession in which the narrative itself originates, when, having begun his report with the words, "It is midnight. The rain is beating on the windows," he wearily concludes:

I lived in the garden. I have spoken of a voice telling me things. I was getting to know it better now, to understand what it wanted. It did not use the words that Moran had been taught when he was little and that he in his turn had taught to his little one. So that at first I did not know what it wanted. But in the end I understood this language. I understood it, I understood it, all wrong perhaps. That is not what matters. It told me to write the report. Does this mean that I am freer now than I was? I do not know. I shall learn. Then

[25] Specifically, Moran's leg begins to stiffen, announcing the loss of the sitting position in subsequent characters. In this connection, it is interesting to note that "to possess" derives from the Latin *possidere*, "to sit as master," "take possession of," "possess," from *posse*, "to be able," and *sedere*, "to sit."

I went back into the house and wrote, It is midnight. The
rain is beating on the windows. It was not midnight. It was
not raining. (*M* 292–93/175–76)

Considered in the light of its subsequent denial, this concluding repetition of the introductory, "It is midnight. The
rain is beating on the windows," clearly suggests that the
story of Moran's dispossession is essentially an allegory of
the dispossession of Moran's story. What Moran's parting
disavowal avows, in other words, is that the sense of his
quest was a quest of sense originating, as its failure alone
would indicate, in the dispossession of sense itself, including most notably that of the first person. Indeed, whether
the first person be here understood as the narrator or as
the reader, the very belatedness of its awakening attests to
the involvement of subjectivity in an economy of signification wherein subjectivity itself unites an "already" or immemorial past, a "not yet" or indefinite futurity, and an
ontological conditionality or "as though." For as I previously remarked, the words, "It is midnight. The rain is
beating on the windows," represent both an end and a beginning: Moran's belated awakening to the sense or sense-
lessness of his quest (to the sense of his quest *as* a quest of
sense), temporally indistinguishable from the substitution
for Youdi of an anonymous voice, is precisely what initiates
the repetition of a pre-originary past in a posthumous
future;[26] and this temporal non-self-coincidence, by virtue
of which Moran the narrator is no longer Moran the character, and the character not yet the narrator, describes the
latent, inactual, illusory, or indeed, allegorical nature of
the first person. Similarly, the words, "It was not midnight.
It was not raining," belatedly alert the reader to her or his

---

[26] It is of course not only in the prose that the paradoxical character of
Beckettian time finds articulation. In *Waiting for Godot* (New York: Grove
Press, 1954; Grove Press Evergreen, 1956), Pozzo muses: "They give
birth astride of a grave, the light gleams an instant, then it's night once
more" (57); while Hamm observes in *Endgame* (New York: Grove Press,
1958): "The end is in the beginning and yet you go on" (69).

own "lost time," to that inevitable misreading which originates in the illusory originarity of sense or meaning, and
simultaneously inaugurate a rereading whose only sense is
the return of this very dispossession. Thus, "It was not
midnight. It was not raining" does not ultimately affirm a
sense more originary than that of the story of Moran's dispossession, to which the latter would then stand as an allegorization of the proper,[27] but rather denies the "propriété" or originarity of sense itself and hence implies that
sense is always yet to come and, in this its very difference,
always allegorical. Whence in fact the paradox or aporia of
these concluding sentences, which purport to mean what
they say at the very moment that they deny the possibility
of so doing and accordingly confirm the dispossession that
conditions all "propriété." To speak (agoreuein) is, therefore, essentially to speak "otherwise" (allegorein)—which is
to say that the only sens or direction of signification is toward the outside already within, in an economy whose only
sameness is the repetition of difference, whose only "propriété" is the return of dispossession, and in which the
voice of the first person turns out never to have been its
own.

.   .   .

In this way, the voice of the first person belatedly bespeaks
the unbelievable reversal of historical time constitutive of
sameness or separation in general, and hence of historical
time itself, and returns us to what I have called, after Derrida, the strange structure of signification or supplemen-

---

[27] It should be clear how the sense of the word "allegorical" as it is used
here differs from the sense to which I alluded in n. 20. The second part
of *Molloy* (to say nothing of the first and of *Malone Dies* and *The Unnamable*) is an allegory, not in the sense that it would refer to an originary
signified but in the sense that it refers to a pre-originary signifier. It is, in
other words, the sign of a sign, the allegory of an allegory. The error
mentioned earlier has to do, not with reference *per se*, but with the assumption that the referent is not itself a sign or a text.

tarity. We have by now seen the effect of this structure at no less than two levels, which it would do well briefly to review before considering the novel and the trilogy as a whole. Thus, within the story itself, what comes first is that embodiment, that figuration or incarnation of subjectivity as separation that is Moran's earthly paradise, the very originarity of which is nevertheless belied by the subsequent intrusion of a messenger annunciating an "already" and a "not yet" to which, indeed, the two parts of the story may be said to correspond.[28] And it is, again, this annunciation that inaugurates the story of Moran's dispossession: as I earlier noted, the incompletion of Gaber's statement at once reverses and reinscribes the temporal reversal by virtue of which separation assumes its illusory priority and so confounds priority itself, awakening Moran to the immemorial originarity of an economy in which his only identity is the confusion with Molloy and committing him to a mission whose only *telos* is the accomplishment of this confusion, the "not yet" of this "already," the fulfillment of a prophetic incompletion. The paradisiacal moment of separation thus proves to be *in medias res*, a moment where, far from "standing out" from each other, as the term *ekstasis* implies, past and future communicate, and whose very non-self-coincidence is characteristic of a temporality that both produces and confounds the historical time of separation.

In the second place, however, and precisely for this reason, any statement regarding the story "itself" necessarily becomes problematic. That Gaber's intrusion inaugurates the story of Moran's dispossession means that this story

---

[28] The instances of what one might call Beckett's mania for spatial symmetry are myriad and would require unto themselves an entire catalogue. They are noteworthy in that they often correspond, as in the case at hand, to a moment of indecision or, as the title *Textes pour rien* suggests, to a "mesure pour rien." As I indicate in the present chapter, however, the moment of indecision is produced by the fundamental dissymmetry of the temporality of signification; it is the moment of repetition par excellence.

originates in the very dispossession of originarity or priority, that is, of historical time itself. In other words, the simultaneous reversal and reinscription of the belated and therefore illusory priority of separation defines not only the first person but the historical time intrinsic to it, as yet to come and hence as other than itself. This in turn not only explains the *fêlure* within the story but, on a larger scale, describes the story *as fêlure,* insofar as its time—*le temps de l'histoire*—is (un)grounded in the reversal made possible by *le temps du récit,* by the differential temporality of signification. Thus, just as the narrator appears to precede his own genesis, so, in the first instance, does the story inevitably appear to preexist its own telling; and just as the narrator's concluding disavowal attests to the illusory nature of his precedence, or, which amounts to the same, to the allegorical nature of his self, so indeed does it imply that the story appears to preexist its telling only because it is already other than itself, so does it suggest that the self of the story is already a differential repetition conditioned by the economy of telling, so, in short, does it testify that the story of the dispossession of the first person necessarily entails the dispossession of the story itself.

Finally, and in keeping with my earlier remarks, we would expect the strange structure of signification or supplementarity at work both within the second part of *Molloy* and, so to speak, in the relation of this part to itself, to provide a model or paradigm for the relation between the two parts of the novel—although, to be sure, the strangeness of this structure is such as to problematize the very notion of paradigm, such, in other words, as to suggest that what is paradigmatic of the series in question is precisely the lack of a paradigm. And indeed, the movement from the story of dispossession to the dispossession of that story initiates a *mise en abîme* in which the originary absence of origin itself defines the latter as always yet to come and that further articulates the relation not only of the second to the first part of the novel but, as I will presently maintain, of *Molloy,* the "origin" of the trilogy, to the trilogy as a whole. For the dispossession of the story of dispossession refers to an economy in which the only sameness of this or any story is its pre-originary difference, or what I have called the relation of the story to itself (a relation that precedes and conditions the self of the story), and in which this relation or difference foretells another, that is, a different or supplementary, story. This foretelling of the supplement corresponds in turn to the strange structure of *Molloy*, the first part of which represents both the "already" and the "not yet" of the second, at once its prologue and its epilogue (the more unmistakably so as the *archē* and the *telos* of Molloy's own failure is that figure of birth and death which is the Mother), and so confounds or dispossesses the *logos* of historical time in whose terms Molloy's story would merely supplement or follow Moran's. Whence the ambiguous pertinence of the examples cited earlier,[29] which attest that the relation between the two parts of *Molloy* can be understood in historical terms only if historical time itself is understood to be both produced and exceeded by the temporality of signification. In other words, Moran's story is originary precisely by virtue of Molloy's—which is to say that Molloy's story functions, not as a more originary origin but as the difference of origin and hence of historical time in general. The simultaneous reversal and inauguration of historical time on the basis of which Moran's story assumes its historical priority is and can only be produced by a temporality in which the moment differs from itself; and to say that the temporality of signification exceeds historical time means that the origin can be what it is, that is, the origin of . . . , only *as* the repetition of its originary difference. To read *Molloy* in historical terms, then, is necessarily to reread it: the structure of this work, according to which the belated origin of historical time bespeaks the return of subjectivity's irrecoverable past in its indefinite future, paradoxically ascribes the irreversibility of historical time itself to the dispossession in which it is (un)grounded. And it is in this sense that one

---

[29] See pp. 40–41, above.

may speak, again, of a *mise en abîme*; for precisely because historical time originates in an irreversible dispossession, the movement from the second to the first part of *Molloy* will appear at once progressive and regressive, will lead simultaneously forward and backward, will parallel an approach of death that literally approximates rebirth. Witness Moran's rebirth in Molloy, who nonetheless remains Moran's own latency, his "already" and his "not yet," insofar as Molloy himself is reborn in his mother: it is only a slip of the tongue and, for Beckett, an entirely plausible one at that, from "my mother's room" to "my mother's womb," and Molloy's physical and mental incapacity ("I've forgotten how to spell too, and half the words" [*M* 8/7], to cite but one example) signal the encroachment of infancy no less than of senility. "I am in my mother's room" (*M* 7/7)—the inaugural sentence of *Molloy* and thus of the trilogy as a whole—describes an anonymous subject who is no longer Molloy and not yet his mother, and whose very anonymity testifies both to the temporal non-self-identity and to the fundamental intersubjectivity of the Beckettian subject. What this further implies, however, is that, if the first part of *Molloy* foretells the dispossession of the second, its own dispossession is foretold by the movement of signification that exceeds or supplements *Molloy* in *Malone Dies* and *The Unnamable*.

It thus remains to state explicitly—albeit briefly, since this cannot be done without anticipating the chapters that follow—the pertinence of this analysis to the relation between *Molloy*, on the one hand, and *Malone Dies* and *The Unnamable*, on the other. The reading of *Molloy* has repeatedly drawn attention to a differential economy in which the historical time of separation is always yet to come and in which, therefore, storytelling seeks an end that can only turn out to be a new beginning. Indeed, as we have seen in the case of Moran, it is at the very moment when signification belatedly produces the consciousness of subjectivity's pre-originary involvement in signification itself that storytelling or writing begins anew: Moran is compelled to tell his story by, and of, that which both invests

62   CHAPTER ONE

and escapes the economy proper to the first person and to
the historical time that is its corollary. Writing thus supplements writing itself as the pre-originary dispossession of
speech, where speech is understood in the sense of subjectivity as consciousness, presence to self, or what I have
called separation. In other words, writing as the return of
dispossession is the repetition of death lived as its own difference or deferral. And this, Beckett's essential affinity
with the Freud of *Jenseits des Lustprinzips*, becomes yet more
explicit in the case of Molloy, who declares at the very beginning: "What I'd like now is to speak of the things that
are left, say my goodbyes, finish dying. They don't want
that" (*M* 7/7). The "they," that anonymous consortium pre-
figuring the entirely disembodied voice(s) of *The Unnamable*, announce a compulsion at once to defer and to repeat,
to repeat the deferral of death or rather death itself *as* deferral. So does Molloy write, as does Malone, who nevertheless appears less compelled to do so than the Unnamable, Molloy, or even Moran, to the extent that storytelling
is for him a game destined to relieve, however ineffec-
tively, the monotony of waiting for death: "While waiting
I shall tell myself stories, if I can. . . . Now it is a game, I
am going to play" (*MM* 8–9/180). And in fact Malone, who
in more than one respect resembles Molloy's mother,[30]

[30] Molloy says of his mother: "I called her Mag, when I had to call her
something. And I called her Mag because for me, without my knowing
why, the letter g abolished the syllable Ma, and as it were spat on it, better
than any other letter would have done. And at the same time I satisfied a
deep and doubtless unacknowledged need, the need to have a Ma, that is
a mother, and to proclaim it, audibly" (*M* 25/17). Malone is the first character of the trilogy (not including Marthe, Moran's maid, and before
Macmann and Mahood) whose proper name begins with the syllable
"ma." As blind, deaf, and mute as Molloy's mother, Malone represents,
even during his surrogate's (Macmann's) pathetic romance with
Moll(oy?), a yet more advanced stage of the desexualization to which Molloy refers: "We were so old, she and I, she had had me so young, that we
were like a couple of old cronies, sexless, unrelated, with the same mem-
ories, the same rancours, the same expectations" (*M* 24/17). And finally,
just as Molloy communicates with his mother by knocking on her skull
(*M* 26-27/18), so Malone first notices his visitor when he feels a violent
blow on the head (*MM* 159/269). It goes without saying that the examples

may be said to occupy a moment at which the communication of past and future most clearly produces a present
that does not pass, and which, in a certain sense, would
make of *Malone Dies* Beckett's *Purgatorio*.[31] Yet not even
Malone escapes "the voice of that silence" (*MM* 48/203)
that compels Moran, Molloy, and the Unnamable to speak,
if only in order to silence that voice by telling the impossible history of silence itself. And the end of *Malone Dies*,

cited here are not meant to establish the *identity* of Malone and Molloy's
mother, but rather to emphasize the possibility and indeed the inevitabil-
ity of metamorphosis and confusion (or substitution) intrinsic to a universe where the subject is always non-self-identical and its properties or
predicates essentially free-floating. In this connection, it is to be noted
that Malone's visitor occupies a position analogous not only to Molloy's
with respect to his mother but, perhaps more fundamentally, to Gaber's
with respect to Moran, to that of "this man who comes every week" (*M* 7/
7) with respect to Molloy and to that of the voice(s) haunting the Unnamable. We have already seen and will see again in the next chapter that the
intersubjective confusion just mentioned necessarily implies a third
whom, in accordance with the irreversibility of dispossession described in
the trilogy, one finds ever more bereft of the status of a character.

[31] Needless to say, the analogy can be pursued only so far. Originally,
that is, when Beckett was composing *Molloy* (see n. 32, below), the moment of purgatory would have corresponded in historical terms to the
first part of this novel. And it is indeed Molloy who says: "Cette fois-ci,
puis encore une je pense, puis c'en sera fini je pense. . . . C'est le sens de
l'avant-dernier" (*M* 9/8); who speaks of his "irréel voyage, pénultième
d'une forme pâlissante entre formes pâlissantes" (*M* 24/16–17); and who
compares himself to Belacqua (*M* 13/10), the character from the fourth
canto of Dante's *Purgatorio* who is condemned to relive his life before
being admitted, first, to purgatory itself, and only later to heaven. (Belacqua lends his name to the hero of *More Pricks Than Kicks* and is alluded
to in *Murphy*, *How It Is*, "The Lost Ones," and "Company.") Yet the reference to Belacqua would imply a quadripartite structure (life, antepur-
gatory, purgatory, heaven [or hell]), which emerges only with *The Unnam-
·able* and of which *Malone Dies* represents the third part. What is to be
retained from all of this, in any case, is precisely the liminal nature of the
moment in Beckett's work: it is the locus of repetition, in which nothing
occurs or in which the moment itself recurs, the product, as I suggest
below, of an asymptotic deferral wherein the infinite contraction of time
is also and at once the infinite dilation of the instant. So does Malone
observe of Macmann: "And perhaps he has come to that stage of his instant when to live is to wander the last of the living in the depths of an
instant without bounds" (*MM* 97/233).

where the end of Malone's final story and that of telling itself ostensibly coincide, just as the death of the story's hero, Macmann, and that of its teller are seemingly one and the same, is in fact no end at all but gives birth to the supplement entitled *The Unnamable*. In the very belatedness of its conception,[32] this volume underscores the irreducibility of the for-itself of signification to the phenomenological understanding of subjectivity; for the concluding "plus rien" (*MM* 191/288) of *Malone meurt*, which may appear to designate a self-coincidence in death, negation, or separation, is exceeded by a simultaneously postmortem and prenatal subjectivity recalling not only the "already" or "no longer" and the "not yet," but also the "comme si," the essentially latent, inactual, illusory, or allegorical character of the for-itself of signification. "I have to speak . . . ," says the Unnamable, "first of the creature I am not, as if I were he, and then, as if I were he, of the creature I am" (*I* 81/335). The irreducibility of the "as if" to the classical alternatives of being and nothingness defines the being of subjectivity as difference: *The Unnamable* gives us to think separation, negation, or death itself as an asymptotic deferral destined to leave that ineliminable excess or residue which Beckett has called "a stain upon the silence,"[33] as an abyssal difference of historical time that leaves the subject of the trilogy, in its own, closing words, eternally on "the threshold of my story" (*I* 213/414).

Thus, the end is also a beginning insofar as the trilogy

---

[32] A systematic comparison of certain passages in the French original and the English translation of *Molloy* would indicate that *The Unnamable* was not planned: "Cette fois-ci, puis encore une je pense, puis c'en sera fini je pense. . . . C'est le sens de l'avant-dernier" (*M* 9)—"This time, then once more I think, then perhaps a last time, then I think it'll be over. . . . Premonition of the last but one but one" (*M* 8); "cet irréel voyage, pénultième d'une forme pâlissante entre formes pâlissantes" (*M* 24)—"that unreal journey . . . the second last but one of a form fading among fading forms" (*M* 16–17); "Oui, crions, cette fois-ci, puis encore une peut-être" (*M* 39)—"Yes, let me cry out, this time, then another time perhaps, then perhaps a last time" (*M* 25), etc.

[33] Quoted in Bair, *Samuel Beckett*, 640.

culminates in a radical reduction of "propriété" that returns subjectivity to the dispossession in which historical time itself originates. As I have remarked more than once, however, this return is not a recovery, and the *temps perdu* is in this sense no more a *temps retrouvé* in Beckett than in Proust. For again, the strangeness of the temporality of signification is such as belatedly to produce a time in which signification itself is misunderstood as belated; and it is a measure not only of subjectivity's pre-originary involvement in signification but of the irreversibility of its dispossession, that the very consciousness of dispossession should require the belated repetition of dispossession itself. So it is that dispossession forces subjectivity to back into its future, like the angel of history in Walter Benjamin's *Über den Begriff der Geschichte*,[34] or as Molloy will suggest in reference to the belated Cartesian, Geulincx: "I . . . had loved the image of old Geulincx, dead young, who left me free, on the black boat of Ulysses, to crawl towards the East, along the deck" (*M* 82/51). Free to crawl east along the deck of a vessel bearing him inexorably west, Molloy figures an experience of history that dispossesses the historical time of subjectivity as separation, and with it, no doubt, the era in which the philosophy of separation has striven to totalize the very alterity that conditions and exceeds it.

---

[34] Walter Benjamin, *Gesammelte Schriften*, ed. Rolf Tiedemann and Hermann Schweppenhäuser (Frankfurt: Suhrkamp, 1977), 1:697–98; "Theses on the Philosophy of History," in *Illuminations*, trans. Harry Zohn, edited and with an introduction by Hannah Arendt (New York: Schocken, 1969), 257–58.

Chapter Two

IMPERSONALITY

Quelqu'un est là, où je suis seul.
—Blanchot

IN THE introduction to this study, I suggested that temporality and intersubjectivity represent the Scylla and Charybdis of phenomenology. In the first chapter, I attempted to state how, in *Molloy*, the "origin" of the trilogy, as well as in *Malone Dies* and *The Unnamable*, the temporality of signification dispossesses the historical time of the first person, and alluded to the pre-originary impersonality of the first person itself. It would do well therefore to begin here by recalling that dispossession, by reason of which the first person, the for-itself or subject originates only as the belated repetition of its pre-originary difference and hence is always already other than or outside of itself, clearly implies a certain intersubjectivity as the precondition of subjectivity as separation, that is, of what Husserl calls "das einsame Seelenleben." This has in fact proven to be a fundamental concern of contemporary thought: for Heidegger's *das Man*, the anonymous, public "they"; Lévinasian *il y a*; Blanchot's theory of impersonality; the Deleuzian *moi passif* and *je fêlé*; Derrida's concept of *écriture*; and the voice(s) haunting the subject(s) of Beckett's trilogy—these are but a few (albeit among the more noteworthy) of the ways in which the twentieth century has sought to think an intersubjective alterity at once constitutive of and irreducible to the phenomenological universe of same and other. Beckett's pertinence to the theoretical preoccupations embodied in the work of such thinkers, and more generally to the historical failure or exhaustion of phenomenology itself, is indeed most readily apparent in his thematization of intersubjectivity, from *Molloy* onward, in terms of the problematic relation between speech and writing. It is to *Molloy* that we briefly return, then, before considering *Malone Dies* and *The Unnamable*.

I have already discussed the temporal significance of these, the final sentences of the second part of *Molloy*: "Then I went back into the house and wrote, It is midnight. The rain is beating on the windows. It was not midnight. It was not raining" (*M* 293/176). This conclusion suggests, again, that the story of Moran's dispossession is an allegory of the dispossession of Moran's story, that the sense of his quest is essentially a quest of sense originating in the dispossession of sense itself. And, as we have seen, this belated awakening to the pre-originary dispossession of "propriété" is in turn temporally indistinguishable from the advent of a voice no longer ascribed to Him on whom, as his name and his status as *patron* imply,[1] the very "propriété" of the story itself ultimately relies. Supervising the "vast organization" (*M* 179/107) of messengers and agents of which Moran is presumably a part, and so founding the world of decision, action, and power in which the Molloy affair, were it not extraordinary, would ordinarily have unfolded, Youdi is the keeper of a *logos* or truth that his subordinate is loath to call into question. Not only does Moran incline to believe that Youdi's Molloy is "the real one [le vrai]" (*M* 192/115), but, in his futile attempt to recall the end or purpose of his mission, he assumes that Youdi originally communicated that mission in a complete and unabridged form and hence that "if, having found Molloy, I still did not know what to do with him, I could always manage to get in touch with Gaber without Youdi's knowing. . . . I would send him a telegram, How deal with

---

[1] Concerning the name Youdi, see chap. 1, above, n. 20. The French word "patron" means not only "chief" or "boss" but, among other things, "pattern" or "model." Youdi may thus be said to constitute a kind of subjective paradigm, and Gaber's statement a prophecy of which Moran's *recherche* would be the mimetic accomplishment.

M?" (*M* 229/138). It is only with the definitive incompletion of his mission and during his return home that Moran
hears a voice neither Gaber's nor Youdi's, and whose own
return is destined to confirm, regarding this transcendental subject and the universe for which he stands, a suspi-
cion harbored even before the hero's departure:

> That we thought of ourselves as members of a vast orga-
> nization was doubtless also due to the all too human feeling
> that trouble shared, or is it sorrow, is trouble something, I
> forget the word. [Si nous nous voyions membres d'un im-
> mense réseau, c'était sans doute aussi en vertu du sentiment
> très humain qui veut que le partage diminue l'infortune.]
> But to me at least, who knew how to listen to the falsetto of
> reason, it was obvious that we were perhaps alone in doing
> what we did. Yes, in my moments of lucidity I thought it pos-
> sible. And, to keep nothing from you, this lucidity was so
> acute at times that I came even to doubt the existence of Ga-
> ber himself. And if I had not hastily sunk back into my dark-
> ness I might have gone to the extreme of conjuring away the
> chief too and regarding myself as solely responsible for my
> wretched existence. . . . And having made away with Gaber
> and the chief (one Youdi), could I have denied myself the
> pleasure of—you know. (*M* 179/107)

So it is that Moran's own dispossession, or rather the dispossession of his story, will encompass this privileged character: Youdi turns out to have been the belated personifi-
cation of a voice belonging, it seems, to no one:

> And the voice I listen to needs no Gaber to make it heard.
> For it is within me and exhorts me to continue to the end the
> faithful servant I have always been, of a cause that is not
> mine, and patiently fulfil in all its bitterness my calamitous
> part. . . . (*M* 219/131–32)

Thus, the voice in question, of which Moran asserts that "it
told me to write the report" (*M* 293/176) and which makes
of him "the faithful servant I have always been," does not
subject him to another subject; and if he serves "a cause

that is not mine," this does not assign the cause, as it were by default, to another self. In this passage as in the conclusion to which I just referred, Moran essentially disavows the very *logos* whereby the dispossession of the first person might be and in fact perennially *is* ascribed to another and a greater power, and alludes to a universe of which the illusory and sedative ontotheology of separation is but a belated effect.

But indeed, the advent of this voice would not commit Youdi's to oblivion did it not also signal the loss of Moran's own. It does so in the precise sense that, while here no less than in Husserl the voice of the first person is the very medium of its temporal self-coincidence, the moment of this advent is the moment at which Moran awakens to the *à venir*, to the *avènement* or advent of an immemorial "already," at which he belatedly understands the only sense of his search for Molloy to be the return of his own perdition. What I have called the dispossession of his story or of the sense of his quest thus amounts, as I suggested in the previous chapter, to the *effondement*[2] of presence or the present, of the "Augenblick" in which subjectivity as separation is grounded. And since the "Augenblick" designates the instant or moment in which subjectivity *simultaneously* ("im selben Augenblick") speaks and hears/understands itself, which therefore harbors the presence both of sense to subjectivity and of subjectivity to itself, which determines, in short, both the sense of subjectivity and the subjectivity of sense *as presence*, its *effondement* also and at once dispossesses the phenomenological voice. What we must recall here, however, is that the phenomenological voice remains, in its very essence, *silent*: "das einsame Seelenleben" is predicated upon the instantaneous self-effacement of the (phonic) sign. It is, then, the dispossession of this same silence that yields, in the words of the Unnamable, "this voice that is not mine, but can only be mine" (*I* 34/307), a

---

[2] The term is used by Deleuze to denote a temporal ungrounding correlative to repetition. See, for example, *Différence et répétition*, 123.

voice belonging neither to the first nor to another person, and which Moran, Molloy, and their successors can in turn appropriate, that is, which they can silence, only by speaking. The belated appropriation of what Malone will call "the voice of that silence" (*MM* 48/203) succeeds, as a result, only in renewing the dispossession of silence itself, in reproducing a voice whose pre-originary "impropriété" defines the pre-originary sense of subjectivity as irreducibly other than that of separation. As we have thus far seen most clearly in the case of Moran, the beginning of this repetition or re-presentation coincides indeed with the return of a voice that compels the hero to reiterate the immemorial loss of his own. The voice in question raises what Blanchot has correctly identified as the central question of the trilogy, to wit: "Who is speaking in Samuel Beckett's novels?"[3] By no accident, the question of who can be said *to speak* arises at the very moment that Moran begins *to write*.

This moment arrives, however, at the end of a report supposedly written by Moran, and in its very belatedness suggests that we shall come no closer to understanding the Beckettian thematization of intersubjectivity in terms of the relation between speech and writing until we approach this relation from a *functional* rather than a *substantial* perspective. For although it goes without saying that Moran's report is written, in the substantial sense of that word, nevertheless the aporia with which this report concludes and which denies the priority of "propriété" in the language of "propriété" itself, indicates the illusory if inevitable originarity of a universe wherein writing as substance is functionally reduced to and hence mistaken for speech. This mistake informs not only the unavoidable misreading of Moran's report, moreover, but—inasmuch as he mistakes it for the speech of their master—Moran's own initial misreading of Gaber's. In both cases, the mistaken functional reduction of writing to speech amounts to an effacement

---

[3] *Le Livre à venir*, 286.

of signification in general that dissimulates the functional non-self-identity of speech itself. And indeed, it is precisely to the functional non-self-identity of *speech* that the conclusion of Moran's report, focusing as it does on the sign itself and momentarily uniting the functional and substantial aspects of *writing*, belatedly draws attention. Writing is therefore to be understood here primarily as the functional difference of *speech*, and only secondarily as the substance in which that difference repeats or supplements itself. We return to the strange structure of supplementarity insofar as, in its very secondarity to the illusory disappearance of the sign in speech, the reappearance of the sign in writing testifies to the pre-originarity of a general economy of signification in which writing and speech are functionally indistinguishable. That the relation between speech and writing corresponds to this structure implies that speech itself is always already a *relation*, that is, a *sign*, and that the only functional sameness of speech is produced through and as the belated repetition of its non-self-identity or difference in the supplement called writing. Thus, writing describes at once the fundamentally figurative character or "impropriété" of speech, whose purported effacement of signification (its "silence") requires the mediation of signification itself (what Beckett has aptly termed "a stain upon the silence"), and the repeatability or iterability that is its essential corollary. As this predominantly functional approach to the relation between speech and writing clearly suggests, to write is, in the trilogy, essentially to speak again.

At the same time, these remarks should have served to indicate that to speak again (*iterare*) is also to speak otherwise (*allegorein*). As Derrida has noted,[4] the prefix "iter-" (from the Sanskrit *itara*, "other") implies a fundamental correlation between repetition and alterity—one that does not, in Husserlian fashion, ground both repetition and alterity in an originary same but rather defines this originary

---

[4] Jacques Derrida, *Marges de la philosophie* (Paris: Minuit, 1972), 375.

same as the repetition of a pre-originary difference. Considered in its temporal dimension, this *différance* explains the belatedness with which arises the question of who can be said to speak; for as we have seen, the very strangeness of differential temporality is such as belatedly to produce that economy of separation proper to the first person in which the pre-originary difference of the first person itself is inevitably misconstrued as belated. Considered in its ontological (and epistemological) dimension, difference here describes the error of this misinterpretation or misunderstanding; for again, just as Moran initially assumes that it is Youdi who "speaks," so does the reader initially assume the same of Moran. To be retained for our present purposes is that the subsequent denial of this fallacious assumption affirms the irreducibility of the question of who can be said to speak to the economy in which the mistaken answer to that question is endowed with an illusory priority to the question itself. In keeping with the general economy of the question, however, which produces that restricted economy of the answer wherein the illusion of sameness is the criterion of all truth, the truth of this illusion can only be told *as* its very repetition. So does Moran remark:

> For it is one of the features of this penance that I may not pass over what is over and straightway come to the heart of the matter. But that must again be unknown to me which is no longer so and that again fondly believed which then I fondly believed, at my setting out. (*M* 221/133)

Moran must, therefore, (re)tell his story as though the voice in question were Youdi's, just as we must (re)read that story as though it were Moran who "speaks." The story itself is, as I have pointed out, an allegory of its own dispossession to the extent that its "propriété" or sameness represents the belated alteration of its very alterity. But the same may of course be said of its subject: Moran "speaks otherwise" insofar as the assumed identity of the narrative "I" repeats the difference, at once ontological and temporal, of a voice not his own—"as if," says the Unnamable, "I were speaking [comme si c'était moi qui parlais]" (*I* 137/ 369). It seems, then, that the question of who can be said to speak in the trilogy, that is, the question of intersubjectivity itself, is opened in the allegorical space of the "as if." We may reformulate an earlier statement—to the effect that the sense of Moran's quest is a quest of sense originating in the dispossession of sense itself—by saying that the subject of this quest(ion) is precisely the quest(ion) of a subject whose fundamental iterability *is* its irreducibility to separation.

The correlation of repetition and alterity implied by this iterability appears to place us on familiar ground; for in the previous chapter, the intersubjective dimension of the trilogy first emerged in a discussion of the temporal relation between Moran and Molloy. There we saw indeed that, inasmuch as he represents both Moran's "already" and his "not yet," Molloy literally evokes or calls forth an intersubjective confusion that dispossesses the separation or presence to self of the first person. Within the story itself, so to speak, the (pseudo)couple Moran-Molloy is of course constituted by a third person or character (Youdi) whose absence in no way calls into question the *logos* of separation as long as it is misunderstood merely as a presence that is elsewhere and that, consequently, sustains the possibility of mistaking Molloy himself, despite the confusion he evokes, for such a presence. Although the dispossession of Moran's story will, to be sure, reveal the person of Youdi to have been a fiction, this fiction remains structurally consonant with the dispossession itself: the voice consigning Youdi's to oblivion occupies a "position" one can only characterize as that of a third. The effect of the dispossession, on the other hand, is precisely to demystify the universe in which this third is misunderstood *as a person* and in which Moran's quest for Molloy amounts to no more than the self's pursuit of another self. It is for this reason that Molloy may be said to evoke what I have named an intersubjective confusion only to the extent that he represents Moran's *own* immemorial alterity and, as such, foretells Moran's sole identity as the repetition of that alterity in a becoming-Molloy. In other words, the proper name Molloy anticipates the Unnamable insofar as it refers to the very confusion of Molloy and Moran and locates both the *archē* and the *telos* of the trilogy in a third that is properly unnamable in the language of separation.

We may in fact equate this third with language itself, provided the latter is defined as the "space between" of an *inter*subjectivity upon whose reduction subjectivity as separation is founded. As we saw in the introduction, this reduction embodies the fundamental paradox of separation: for while it presumably constitutes subjectivity as an identity that is the condition of possibility of its own repetition, this very repetition remains a possibility only if subjectivity is pre-originarily non-self-identical. The fundamentally paradoxical character of a subjectivity whose sameness is born in the repetition of its pre-originary difference bespeaks the immemorial *effondement* of separation in an economy where, by reason of the other of separation always already within, subjectivity is always already without, where the phenomenological *pour-soi* is the *pour l'autre* of signification, where the personal pronoun "I" (or *ego*) stands for or takes the place of an impersonal "it" (or *ille*, if not *id*).[5] "Put *for itself*, instead of itself,"[6] the first person signifies a "self" that is none other than its own alterity— which is to say that the only meaning of the pronoun "I" resides in the sameness *of* its difference, and that the allegorical place or space of subjectivity is neither inside nor yet simply outside but in the other of their very separation. What must be stressed here, however, is that the very pre-

[5] Readers of Lévinas will recognize the close relation of such notions as "autrui," "illéité," and "il y a" to the intersubjective "il(s)" of Beckett's trilogy. Moreover, the impersonality to which all of these terms refer is not unrelated to a certain understanding of the unconscious as a dimension beyond being and nothingness that escapes consciousness as it produces it. See also chap. 1, n. 4, above.

[6] Derrida, *VP* 99/89.

originarity of this other defines the relation between the
general economy of signification and the restricted economy of separation as essentially dissymmetrical: that the
pre-originary non-self-identity of subjectivity constitutes
the condition of possibility of its repetition and hence of its
identity means that subjectivity as separation is indeed *conditioned* by a universe in which separation and its predicates—most notably, in this context, the freedom and the
power *not* to speak—do not obtain. Earlier encountered
precisely in its correlation to temporal dissymmetry, the
conditionality of separation refers to a dimension of Beckett's trilogy that these preliminary remarks on the thematization of intersubjectivity in terms of the relation, itself
dissymmetrical, between writing and speech, now leave us
better prepared to discuss. While confirming the irreducibility of the question of who can be said to speak to any
possible answer, and thereby suggesting that every answer
effects in fact a return of the question itself, this conditionality provides the basis for an explanation of why the
quest(ion) of an answer—of silence—is experienced as
both an impossibility and a necessity. It not only recalls the
texts of Blanchot, Lévinas, and Heidegger, of Deleuze and
Derrida, but also underscores, as I shall presently maintain, the communication of Beckettian intersubjectivity
with Bataillian *expérience* and with Freud's inspiration, at its
most radical, in *Jenseits des Lustprinzips*.

. . .

As a prelude to the following discussion concerning certain predicates of differential intersubjectivity, it would no
doubt do well to forestall a common misunderstanding
that derives from the persistence of separation itself in the
effort to think its other. In the case at hand, this misunderstanding would consist of thinking that the words
"speech" and "writing" mean what they say, that we are
concerned with speech and writing in their proper sense.
Their proper sense is, to be sure, what one inevitably ap-

pears to invoke when referring to the *thematization* of intersubjectivity in terms of the relation between speech and
writing. The analysis of the relation itself leads one nevertheless to adopt, as we have seen, a functional rather than
a substantial or thematic perspective, a perspective in
which speech and writing are functionally indistinguishable, in which the relationality of the sign *in general* precedes the separation of speech and writing as terms. What
this implies for the thematization is, of course, a dispossession of which *The Unnamable*, more than *Molloy* or *Malone
Dies*, states an explicit awareness, as when its eponymous
hero remarks: "But it's entirely a matter of voices, no other
metaphor is appropriate [Mais c'est entièrement une question de voix, toute autre métaphore est impropre]" (*I* 64/
325).[7] That the metaphor of voice should be considered
proper, as it were, to a literary work that so clearly focuses
on the nature of language itself is hardly surprising; that
it remains a metaphor suggests the converse of an earlier
statement to the effect that to write is essentially to speak
again, namely, that speech itself is always already a "writing." Needless to say, "writing" too is a metaphor; yet it no
longer stands as the figure of an originary "propriété"
called speech but rather designates a general metaphoricity that conditions the separation of the proper and the
figurative. Derrida's use of the word "writing" to describe
this metaphoricity is largely strategic, resulting from the
movement of reversal and reinscription by virtue of which
the devalorized term of a hierarchical opposition comes to
name the other of the opposition itself. In their thematization of a single functional non-self-identity, "writing" so
understood and speech in its Beckettian sense are in fact
equally proper or improper. As metaphors, both refer to
the discursive economy that produces and exceeds them
and in which their only identity is their differential in-

---

[7] While Beckett's translation of "impropre" is perfectly appropriate, it
does not convey the word play of the French, in which "impropre," itself
understood figuratively, ends up calling attention to the figurative nature
of the voice just exempted from figuration.

volvement with other terms. So it is that the impersonal voice(s) haunting the Beckettian subject, as a metaphor of intersubjectivity, afford(s) access to the intertextual relation of Beckett's work with others, such as Freud's or Bataille's, in which intersubjectivity is not *thematized* primarily in terms of language.

This is not to say that there are no points of thematic convergence between Freud and Bataille, on the one hand, and Beckett, on the other. It remains nevertheless that, among the various figures whom one may associate with differential thought, perhaps none tend to thematize intersubjectivity in terms—those of sexuality or, more broadly, the erotic—seemingly more distant from those of Beckett than do Freud and Bataille. Moreover, the frequently exuberant tone of Bataille's work does not appear to recommend comparison with Beckett's rather somber irony. As the previous remarks imply, however, the basic affinity between these three thinkers resides in a functional similarity that characterizes their thematically and stylistically divergent descriptions of intersubjectivity. Indeed, while it entails a rather extended discussion, the choice of Bataille and Freud is motivated to no small degree by the very capacity of this divergence to underscore this similarity, and to suggest in so doing how broad is Beckett's pertinence to any understanding of the general economy. Thus, in an inspiration reminiscent of Beckett's own, both Bataille and Freud define subjectivity *as* the involvement with an impersonal outside. In both cases, the necessity of this definition manifests itself in the *effect* of an economy irreducible to that of separation: for Freud, as we shall see, in a repetition compulsion that confounds any opposition of the pleasure and the reality principles, of the death and the life instincts; for Bataille, in activities that exceed the logic he qualifies, in the early text, "La Notion de dépense," as that of utility, and in the later text entitled *L'Erotisme*, as that of work.[8]

---

[8] Of such activities, Bataille offers the following suggestive list: "luxury,

Since "utility" and "work" do indeed designate one and the same logic, the texts in which they are respectively privileged may be said to represent but two moments of Bataille's sustained effort to think this logic in terms of that which exceeds it, that is, in the terminology of "La Notion de dépense," to think the restricted in terms of the general economy. In *L'Erotisme*, one of Bataille's more accomplished and certainly one of his more well-known works, the priority of the general with respect to the restricted economy finds expression in the essentially dissymmetrical relation between "continuity" and "discontinuity." Discontinuity is first strategically defined in the context of phenomena that are among the more likely to reveal its conditionality, namely, reproduction and death:

> Reproduction brings into play *discontinuous* beings.
>
> Beings that reproduce themselves are distinct from one another and beings reproduced are distinct among themselves as they are distinct from those of which they are born. Each being is distinct from all others. Its birth, its death and the events of its life may have an interest for others, but it alone is directly interested. It alone is born. It alone dies. Between one being and another, there is an abyss, there is a discontinuity.[9]

---

mourning, war, cults, the construction of sumptuary monuments, games, spectacles, arts, perverse sexual activity (i.e., deflected from genital finality) . . . " ("La Notion de dépense," 28; "The Notion of Expenditure," in *Visions of Excess: Selected Writings, 1927–1939*, trans. Allan Stoekl, with Carl R. Lovitt and Donald M. Leslie, Jr., ed. Allan Stoekl [Minneapolis: University of Minnesota Press, 1985], 118). These "so-called unproductive expenditures" are distinguished from the expenditures required by and hence reducible to the restricted economy.

[9] Georges Bataille, *L'Erotisme* (Paris: Minuit, 1957), 18–19; *Erotism: Death and Sensuality*, trans. Mary Dalwood (San Francisco: City Lights, 1986), 12. All further references to this work (henceforth *E*) will be given in the text and will include first the page number of the French edition and second, for the convenience of the reader, the page number of the English translation. The discrepancies between this translation and my own are wide enough that I shall here assume sole responsibility for the English rendering of Bataille's text.

Although this discontinuity or distinction *between beings* pertains to all reproductive organisms (including the asexual), its specifically human dimension is understood, here as in Blanchot,[10] to be the corollary of a separation *from being*: the negation or transformation of nature through work describes the transition from animality to humanity wherein the discontinuity "brought into play" by reproduction (to say nothing of death) assumes the institutionalized form of *interdits* or prohibitions that in turn negatively define the restricted economy of work and the principal value in whose service it stands, to wit, the conservation of life.[11] While Bataille readily concedes that the inception of work and the imposition of prohibitions concerning sexuality and death remain inaccessible as historical events, he also maintains that they are essentially contemporaneous and very much of a piece:

> They [men] distinguished themselves from animals through *work*. Together with this, they imposed on themselves restrictions known as *prohibitions*. These prohibitions essentially— and certainly—concerned attitudes toward the dead. It is probable that they affected at the same time—or toward the same time—sexual activity. (*E* 36/30)

In short, "the totality of fundamental *human* comportments—work, awareness of death, restrained sexuality— date[s] back to the same remote period." (*E* 36/30). Work and the prohibitions that accompany it constitute a world whose *raison d'être* or *telos* is none other than life itself *as discontinuity*. Yet, while it is clear that all forms of that destructive violence proscribed by what Bataille calls *l'interdit lié à la mort*, as well as all forms of "perverse sexual activity (i.e., deflected from genital finality),"[12] call into question

---

[10] See above, pp. 8–9, and the appendix of *L'Espace littéraire* (337–40) entitled "La Solitude essentielle et la solitude dans le monde."

[11] The "conservation" of life includes, of course, its reproduction, but also its expansion. The restricted economy is both conservative and imperialistic.

[12] "La Notion de dépense," 28; "The Notion of Expenditure," 118.

the integrity of this world, the same cannot immediately and without qualification be said of reproduction. Indeed, one would sooner think that, inasmuch as it has as its end the (re)production of discontinuous beings, this sexual activity remains fundamentally in agreement with the restricted economy.[13] Bataille notes, however, that "if it is true that erotism is defined by the independence of erotic pleasure from reproduction as an end, the fundamental sense of reproduction is nonetheless the key to erotism" (*E* 18/12); and the persuasive power of his thought derives in large part from its capacity to detect at the very heart of the restricted economy of discontinuity that which the misleading perspective of this economy construes as a threat from without. It is therefore, as I have suggested, in Bataille's understanding of reproduction that we may expect to discover the dissymmetrical relation between continuity and discontinuity.

The notion of continuity is nevertheless introduced precisely from the perspective of discontinuity, which, as we have seen, holds discontinuity, distinction, or separation and life itself to be synonymous. Hence: "For us, who are discontinuous beings, death has the sense of the continuity of being: reproduction leads to the discontinuity of beings, but it brings into play their continuity, that is, it is intimately related to death" (*E* 19/13). From the point of view of discontinuity, which Bataille often calls a lie ("mensonge") or illusion ("leurre"), the relation between discontinuity and continuity, life and death, is itself inevitably (mis)construed as discontinuous. The inadequacy of a vi-

---

[13] As I note below, it is, for Bataille, the erotic component of reproduction itself that accounts for the prohibitions to which it is subject. Thus, for example, Bataille will maintain against Lévi-Strauss that the prohibition of incest is related only secondarily to the necessity of insuring a certain distribution of women and finds its source in "an incompatibility between the sphere of calm and rational behavior and the violence of the sexual impulse," in "the need to bind with rules a violence that, left free, could have disturbed the order to which the collectivity desired to submit itself" (*E* 61, 59/53, 52).

sion grounded in distinction or separation announces itself in Bataille's rigorously paradoxical characterization of reproduction, which may be reformulated as follows: if reproduction leads to life as discontinuity, its condition of possibility remains a continuity that, for the individual discontinuous being, spells death. As he later observes: "The death of the one is correlative to the birth of the other, which it announces and of which it is the condition" (*E* 62/ 55). What this means is that the relation between life and death, discontinuity and continuity, cannot adequately be understood from the point of view of the individual discontinuous being. The *mise en jeu* of continuity is stressed both in the context of asexual reproduction, where the creation of two discontinuous beings is predicated upon the death, as discontinuity, of their scissiparous progenitor, and where the passage from one to another state of discontinuity "implies between the two an *instant* of continuity" (*E* 20/14); and in the context of sexual reproduction, where the union of two discontinuous cells yields a new, equally discontinuous being that nevertheless "bears within it the transition to continuity, the fusion, fatal for each of them, of the two distinct beings" (*E* 20/14). Moreover, Bataille maintains that the difference, in this respect, between the most elementary and the more complex levels of sexual reproduction is one of degree rather than of kind:

> Those which reproduce survive the birth of those they engender, but this survival is only a reprieve. A stay is granted, partly devoted to helping the newcomers, but the appearance of these newcomers betokens the disappearance of their predecessors. While the reproduction of sexual beings does not lead immediately to death, it does so in the long run. (*E* 111/100–101)

The point to be retained—and the reason for which reproduction represents the key to the erotic—is that the continuity of being or being as continuity, which stands at the origin of all discontinuous beings, spells their death inso-

far as it embodies *the excess of life itself over discontinuity.*
States Bataille: "Life is in its essence an excess, it is the
prodigality of life" (*E* 96/86). Born of and thus conditioned
by the continuity that exceeds it, discontinuity cannot subsequently but exceed itself: "le sens fondamental de la reproduction" is both the direction of a being centrifugally
impelled toward the very outside that, in its excessive investment of interiority, produces the impulsion itself, and
the meaning of this movement, in which the pre-originary
confusion of death and birth defines the life of the discontinuous being as the experience of its own mortality. Death
is not, then, the opposite of life, any more than continuity
represents the negation of discontinuity; rather, "continuity" and "death" designate an economy wherein life itself
is precisely the violation of discontinuity. Reproduction
does not so much involve two discontinuous beings with
each other as it involves each of them with the other of
discontinuity in what Bataille calls, paradoxically, *l'expérience intérieure.* The experience of an interiority impelled
toward the outside in which it originates includes a *dépense*
or expenditure from which the discontinuous being does
not ultimately profit. In other words, reproduction affords
access to the erotic to the extent that, requiring of the reproductive being what is, for the latter, an absolute dispossession or loss, "la *perte* de son avoir" (*E* 106/96), it provides
a model for all those activities which exceed the restricted
economy of utility. Considered as an end, reproduction itself is apparently recuperated by this economy; yet the life
to which it leads must be viewed, from the perspective of
the individual discontinuous being, as "impersonal
growth" (*E* 106/96). And just as reproduction affords access to the erotic in general, so does its essential impersonality inform Bataille's general conception of intersubjectivity.
    As I have pointed out, the specifically human dimension
of discontinuity is predicated upon a separation from or
negation of being effected through work, on the one hand,
and through prohibitions or *interdits,* on the other. The va-

lidity of reproduction as a model for the erotic, that is, for the transgression of these prohibitions, is in no way weakened by the claim that, were one to move from the level of the individual to that of the collective, its essential impersonality for the individual would, so to speak, be humanized by the social group in question; for at stake in reproduction is an excess that calls into question discontinuity as such, whether individual or collective, and including the very distinction between them.[14] Indeed, while its end may be sanctioned by the restricted economy, "the fundamental sense of reproduction" remains that of an activity pursued, as is any distinctly erotic comportment, *for itself*—to an end irreducible to the *telos* of the restricted economy— and that, for this very reason, is subject to a host of prohibitions. The existence of these or of other prohibitions presumably testifies, again, to a negation of the violence that is their common object, to what Bataille terms "man's 'no' to nature" (*E* 68/61). However, the no less remarkable instances of their transgression clearly indicate a violence that exceeds this negation—and does so, as Bataille repeatedly insists, because it originarily invests negation itself. The origin of negation or prohibition in a force that exceeds it explains why transgression is not simply the negation of a negation, "is not animal violence" (*E* 73/64) but rather an *organized, human violence*—is not, in brief, a "return to nature": "transgression is not the same as a 'return to nature': it suspends prohibition without suppressing it" (*E* 42/36). Bataille's use of an explicitly Hegelian vocabulary is here all the more noteworthy given the irreducibility of the relation between prohibition and transgression to a

---

[14] "Collective" discontinuity is, of course, a metaphor, based on the consideration of the collectivity as a single "body." My point here is simply this: although, on the collective level, excess may be more convincingly thematized by an activity such as war, a portion of the expenditure—*la part maudite*—involved in reproduction itself represents an irrecuperable loss *both* for the individual *and* for the social group of which it is a member.

dialectic grounded in negation.[15] Born of excess, prohibition necessarily exceeds itself and does not therefore negate, but rather collaborates with, transgression. This is not, of course, to deny the effective reality of the restricted economy; it is instead a matter of accounting for this reality, as well as for those activities which neither abide by its founding principle nor suffer its claim to totalization, in terms of the general economy that produces the one and the others. The differential constitution of prohibition describes the fundamental complicity or, in a distinctively Lévinasian terminology, the "non-allergic" relation between prohibition and transgression, in which prohibition solicits, indeed *requires* transgression, and to which Bataille refers in the proposition: " 'The prohibition is there to be violated' " (*E* 72/64). In other words, prohibition defines itself only in and through transgression. Observes Bataille: "The remarkable thing about sexual prohibition is that it is fully revealed in transgression" (*E* 119/107). The "revelation" of this or of any prohibition is not, however, that of an object manifesting itself to consciousness by virtue of the interval that is negation or separation, since the condition of this "revelation" is precisely the transgression of separation itself. The self-transgression of prohibition must accordingly be characterized as that "of which one cannot be conscious (as a transcending intentionality), and of which one cannot but be conscious (as a subjection to a proximity which approaches by virtue of its investment of interiority)."[16] What this means is that transgression, the

---

[15] In a note that fails to elucidate what it portrays as self-evident, namely, the problematic influence of Hegel, Bataille says: "There is no need to stress the Hegelian character of this operation, which corresponds to the moment of the dialectic described by the untranslatable German verb 'aufheben' (surpass while preserving) [dépasser en maintenant]" (*E* 42/36).

[16] Libertson, *Proximity*, 40. Libertson refers in fact to the *il y a* in Lévinas. The pertinence of this remark to the experience of intersubjectivity not only in Bataille but also in Blanchot certainly confirms the intertextual communication to which Libertson's work is devoted. However, the implicit claim made here is that it applies as well to the experience of

involvement with an outside already within, produces a consciousness that remains necessarily inadequate to this involvement.[17] The essentially affirmative dimension of this inadequation is variously described as a *"feeling of self"* irreducible to a "consciousness of self [that] follows upon consciousness of external objects" (*E* 110/99–100), as an *expérience intérieure* that is also and at once an *"hors de soi"* (*E* 114/103), and as a *"pour soi"* (*E* 110/99) assimilable to the unconscious—all of which terms designate the excess of subjectivity over consciousness in a general economy of difference that itself exceeds the restricted economy of separation. That this excess is also a condition explains why the fundamentally conservative world of utility or work is impelled toward an expenditure or loss proportionate to its own growth: the conditionality of the restricted economy *is* in fact the univocity of a movement whose force increases as does the very effort to restrict it. For subjectivity, be it "collective" or "individual," the experience of this conditionality, of this dissymmetry or nonreciprocity, assumes the form of a compulsion and an impossibility that both invest and exceed the power and the freedom born of separation, the form of an *inability not* to transgress its own limits. Transgression is not a liberation, for it does not rely on the power of a negation that would abolish prohibition but reveals the negation that prohibition purportedly represents to be the ineliminable exigency of transgression itself. Transgression leads beyond negation or separation, to a "beyond" that is not the "au-delà" of a transcendental subject but the "ici bas" or "here below" of a subject constitutively intersubjective, of a *pour-soi* essentially *hors de soi*, of an impersonal other always al-

---

intersubjectivity in the trilogy and hence draws Beckett into this group of thinkers who steadfastly refused the phenomenological reductionism that defined the intellectual climate of their generation.

[17] The term "inadequate" is used here in the strictest sense: consciousness is "inadequate" to this involvement to the extent that this involvement is irreducible to a subject-object correlation, to the adequation of consciousness and phenomenal exteriority.

ready within. Bataillian subjectivity is indeed a subjection, a suffering, a passion—the passion of a human being inextricably involved with an impersonal other none other than itself.

As with Bataille, so with Freud my intention is to focus, even at the risk of oversimplification or, given the functional emphasis of this discussion, at the risk of excessive formalization, primarily if not exclusively on those elements of pertinence to the interpretation of Beckettian (inter)subjectivity. I hope to show, through a brief reading of *Jenseits des Lustprinzips*, how, despite thematic or substantive preoccupations apparently quite distant from Beckett's, Freud ends up problematizing closure or separation in a way functionally analogous to Beckett's own and capable of affording a broader comprehension of the context in which Beckett's text must be situated.

In his effort to account for a compulsion to repeat "beyond the pleasure principle," Freud pursues an approach whose similarity to Bataille's is more than nominal:

> In the theory of psycho-analysis we have no hesitation in assuming that the course taken by mental events is automatically regulated by the pleasure principle. We believe, that is to say, that the course of those events is invariably set in motion by an unpleasurable tension, and that it takes a direction such that its final outcome coincides with a lowering of that tension—that is, with an avoidance of unpleasure or a production of pleasure. In taking that course into account in our consideration of the mental processes which are the subject of our study, we are introducing an economic point of view into our work.[18]

The point of view so introduced is "economic" in that it concerns itself with the production and subsequent regu-

[18] Sigmund Freud, *Jenseits des Lustprinzips*, in *Gesammelte Werke*, ed. Anna Freud et al. (London: Imago, 1940), 13:3; *Beyond the Pleasure Principle*, trans. and ed. James Strachey (New York: Norton, 1961), 1. This work will hereafter be cited in the text as *JL*, followed by page references to the German original and, after a slash, to the English translation.

lation or management of tension, that is, of a disequilibrium in the distribution of excitation or energy. It should
of course be noted that this disequilibrium is originary insofar as by it is "set in motion" ("angeregt") the course of
mental events. Furthermore, Freud is quick to point out
that tension and the feelings of unpleasure and pleasure
initially involve "unbound" excitation:

> We have decided to relate pleasure and unpleasure to the
> quantity of excitation that is present in the mind but is not
> in any way bound; and to relate them in such a manner that
> unpleasure corresponds to an increase in the quantity of ex-
> citation and pleasure to a diminution. (*JL* 4/1–2)

From the outset, then—in the primary process specific to
the id and characterized by the presence of unbound excitation alone—pleasure is understood as a discharge of
energy *conditioned* by its very excess. That this discharge or
dépense is but a "diminution" ("Verringerung"), that the expenditure of energy which is pleasure remains inferior to
its investment, may help to explain why Freud predicates
unpleasure of the disequilibrium qualified as originary yet
more pointedly defines this disequilibrium as a pure difference in terms of which the purely differential or relative values of unpleasure and pleasure are determined.
And although this difference implies, in its turn, a resistance that impedes or defers an expenditure equivalent to
the investment itself, it also describes pleasure as a *dépense*
that reduces excess only by virtue of its repetition.[19] As

---

[19] I must point out that the brevity of this *exposé* precludes an adequately detailed discussion of Freud's thought. In the topographical
model proposed in the *Entwurf einer Psychologie* and whose basic structure
is restated in *Jenseits des Lustprinzips*, Freud includes between the systems
designated φ and ψ (which correspond respectively to the outside and the
inside of the mental apparatus, to perception and memory, and both of
which function in a purely *quantitative* way), a third system (consciousness), designated ω, in which quantitative difference becomes *qualitative*
by virtue of the capacity of ω neurons to register temporal differences,
that is, periods of excitation. It is clear that a fuller study of repetition
would require consideration of this topographical feature. See Sigmund

Freud notes in the *Entwurf einer Psychologie* of 1895,[20] the difference between investment and expenditure constitutes a reserve (*Vorrat*) that, while evidently reflecting the quantitative inferiority of pleasure, leads nevertheless, upon reinvestment, to an increased capacity for tension and hence for pleasure as its "outcome" ("Endergebnis"). Indeed, the direction (*Richtung*) to which he alludes in the first quotation above denotes, fundamentally, the lowering or reduction of tension *relative to its univocal increase*. However, since this direction is established only through the repetition of an originary difference, it appears that the pleasure principle itself is basically belated. The "turning point of the twenties," embodied most notably in *Jenseits des Lustprinzips* but clearly prefigured in the *Entwurf einer Psychologie*, may be related to the (re)assertion that binding (*Bindung*), normally construed as effecting the transition from the pleasure to the reality principle, in fact precedes, founds, and conditions the former. "This is what is meant, firstly, by *Beyond the Pleasure Principle*," says Deleuze, "not at all exceptions to this principle, but on the contrary the determination of the conditions under which pleasure actually becomes a principle."[21] Freud himself observes, in a statement that nevertheless bears emendation:

> Only after the binding has been accomplished would it be possible for the dominance of the pleasure principle (and of its modification, the reality principle) to proceed unhindered. Till then the other task of the mental apparatus, the task of mastering or binding excitations, would have precedence—not, indeed, in opposition to the pleasure principle,

---

Freud, *Aus den Anfängen der Psychoanalyse* (London: Imago, 1950), 371–466 (*Project for a Scientific Psychology*, in *The Complete Psychological Works of Sigmund Freud*, trans. and ed. James Strachey [London: Hogarth, 1966], 1:295–387) and Derrida, *L'Ecriture et la différence*, 293–340 (*Writing and Difference*, 196-231).

[20] *Aus den Anfängen der Psychoanalyse*, 385; *Complete Psychological Works*, 1:301.

[21] *Différence et répétition*, 128.

but independently of it and to some extent in disregard of it. (*JL* 36/29)

In short, "binding is a preparatory act which introduces and assures the dominance of the pleasure principle" (*JL* 67/56)—to which one must add, however, that the pleasure principle does not preexist the process of binding, only therewith to achieve its purported dominance; rather, as I have suggested, binding precedes, founds, and conditions pleasure *as principium*—as a supposedly originary regulatory mechanism—and, precisely for this reason, proceeds "independently of it and to some extent in disregard of it." The "independence" of binding accounts for the compulsive character of a repetition that Freud underscores in the well-known case of a child playing "fort-da" no less than in traumatic neuroses, for binding itself is essentially the reinvestment or recathexis of an originary "facilitation" (*Bahnung*), of the path or passage opened by an originary investment differentially superior to the resistance to it. No doubt, the game of "fort-da" may appear to be motivated by a pleasure already obtained or yet to be obtained, although Freud remarks that "the first act, that of departure, was staged as a game in itself and far more frequently than the episode in its entirety, with its pleasurable ending" (*JL* 13/10); or the game of "fort-da" and the dreams occurring in traumatic neuroses may appear to represent an effort retrospectively to master an originary passivity. Yet it is clear, from the very repetition of this game as well as from the recurrence of these dreams, that the production of pleasure or the avoidance of unpleasure do not exhaust the excess by which they are conditioned, and hence that the apparent *telos* of the pleasure principle is exceeded by repetition as the compulsive for-itself of difference. Contrary to what Freud implies above, to bind (*binden*) is not to master (*bewältigen*) but to represent the failure of mastery—in dreams, for example, or indeed, in literature—to affirm sameness of the difference that impels binding itself, of a force irreducible to the sameness of representation and that, in the words of Goethe aptly cited by Freud, "ungebändigt immer vorwärts dringt" (*JL* 45/ 36).

As these remarks are meant to suggest, the basic thrust of *Jenseits des Lustprinzips* calls into question the oppositional or conflictive dualism structuring the totality of Freud's corpus and resolutely reaffirmed even in this, arguably the most ambitious and radical of his metapsychological works.[22] The inevitable and considerable difficulty one encounters in reading this text derives from the tension between an evident tendency to retain the established and familiar system of bipolarities grounded in separation and a more essential, differential tendency to which the vocabulary of that system remains entirely inadequate. We have seen that the originary difference between investment and expenditure defines "unbound" as the *différance* of its own distinction or separation from "bound" excitation. At the same time, this *différance* plainly problematizes the very notion of originarity, and therewith the distinction between the "primary" and the "secondary" processes.[23] And finally, the difference between investment and expenditure ascribes to pleasure as *principium* the reserve as well as the postponement (*Aufschub*) ordinarily associated with the reality principle alone. This is certainly not to say that the reality principle does not differ from or modify the pleasure principle, but rather that the differential constitution of the pleasure principle itself and of the reality principle that it engenders describes their relation as irreducible to conflict or opposition. And Freud says as much when he declares of the reality principle that it supersedes the pleasure principle "without abandoning the intention of ultimately obtaining pleasure" (*JL* 6/4). In

---

[22] "Our views have from the very first been *dualistic*, and today they are even more definitely dualistic than before . . ." (*JL* 57/47).

[23] Both Deleuze and Derrida emphasize the extent to which Freud's own thinking of difference places originarity or "primarity" in question. See *Différence et répétition*, 128–41, and *L'Ecriture et la différence*, 297–305 (*Writing and Difference*, 200–205).

his metapsychology, to whose full complexity it is of course impossible to do justice here and which, in addition to its economic perspective, includes dynamic and topographical points of view, the advent of this principle (which in fact does not supersede but constitutes only a "region" of the pleasure principle), effected through reality-testing (*Realitätsprüfung*), parallels the momentous topographical distinction between ego and id, self and nonself, inside and outside, itself correlative to a dynamic transformation whereby the highly systematized, totalized, or unified cathexis called the ego allows of such operations, destined to maintain that distinction, as repression and inhibition, and corresponding, from the economic perspective, to the transition from a *passive differentiation* to an *active organization* of excess. Here, indeed, one might very well propose an analogy according to which the reality principle is to the pleasure principle in Freud as, in Bataille, prohibition is to discontinuity. For our purposes, however, the communication of Bataille with Freud and of both with Beckett might better be formulated in terms common to them all, in terms, that is, of life and death.

In positing a correlation between the compulsion to repeat and the instincts or drives, Freud proposes the following definition of an instinct: "*It seems, then, that an instinct is an urge inherent in organic life to restore an earlier state of things*" (*JL* 38/30). What is perhaps most noteworthy here is the singular "an instinct" ("ein Trieb"), which of course does not rule out a plurality of instincts but sooner attributes to any and all a single goal or aim, namely, the "restoration of an earlier state of things." Presumably, the aim-inhibited (*zielgehemmt*) character of instinctual behavior results from a conflict or opposition concerning the means to that end. Indeed, Freud repeatedly claims that the death and the life instincts are *opposed*,[24] to the extent that the

---

[24] "[The life instincts] operate against the purpose of the other instincts, which lead, by reason of their function, to death; and this fact indicates that there is an opposition [Gegensatz] between them and the other instincts" (*JL* 43/34); "Our views have from the very first been *du-*

former demand an immediate return "to the quiescence of
the inorganic world" (*JL* 68/56), whereas the latter, "whose
function it is to assure that the organism shall follow its
own path to death, and to ward off any possible ways of
returning to inorganic existence other than those which
are immanent in the organism itself" (*JL* 41/33), are
obliged, because of such possibilities, because of "external
disturbing and diverting influences" (*JL* 39/32), to resist
precisely that which would favor an immediate return.
The opposition between the death instincts and the life instincts thus comes to reflect—their frequent confusion in
Jenseits des Lustprinzips notwithstanding[25]—the opposition
between, on the one hand, what is called, in the *Entwurf
einer Psychologie*, the principle of inertia (*Prinzip der Neuro-
nenträgheit* or *Trägheitsprinzip*), and in *Jenseits des Lustprinzips*, the Nirvana principle, that is, a function whose purpose is the total evacuation or at least a maximal reduction
of excitation, and on the other hand, what is called the
principle of constancy, which denotes a function whose
purpose coincides, not with a total evacuation of excitation
but with its maintenance at a certain level or magnitude.
As the foregoing observations on the genesis of the pleasure principle indicate, however, neither of these principles, in its purported opposition to the other, suffices to

---

alistic, and today they are even more definitely dualistic than before—now
that we describe the opposition as being, not between ego-instincts and
sexual instincts but between life instincts and death instincts [seitdem wir
die Gegensätze nicht mehr Ich- und Sexualtriebe, sondern Lebens- und
Todestriebe benennen]" (*JL* 57/47).

[25] "The dominating tendency of mental life, and perhaps of nervous
life in general, is the effort to reduce, to keep constant or to remove internal tension due to stimuli (the 'Nirvana principle', to borrow a term
from Barbara Low)—a tendency which finds expression in the pleasure
principle; and our recognition of that fact is one of our strongest reasons
for believing in the existence of death instincts" (*JL* 60/49–50); "The pleasure principle, then, is a tendency operating in the service of a function
whose business it is to free the mental apparatus entirely from excitation
or to keep the amount of excitation in it constant or to keep it as low as
possible. We cannot yet decide with certainty in favour of any of these
ways of putting it" (*JL* 67–68/56).

explain the "course of mental events": the relative or differential nature of pleasure wholly invalidates a Nirvana
principle that would not be always already aim-inhibited,
and the univocal increase in tension defines the goal of the
principle of constancy as a ceaselessly re-equilibrated disequilibrium. Yet the inadequacy of opposition appears the
more glaring in the case of the instincts—"the most abun-
dant sources of this *internal* excitation . . . the representatives of all the forces originating in the *interior* of the body
and transmitted to the mental apparatus" (*JL* 35/28, my
emphasis)—as Freud derives it from forces external to the
organism. Thus, his proposal to convert metaphysics into
metapsychology,[26] on the grounds that the former represents a projection of the unconscious, an externalization of
the properly internal, would here fall victim to metaphysics itself. It would be a mistake nevertheless, and a properly metaphysical one at that, to suppose that the correc-
tion of this error would require no more than its
symmetrical reversal; for although the instincts remain, in
a sense presently to be determined, "internal" to the organism, metapsychology describes them as spanning the
frontier between a certain outside and a certain inside, between the soma and the psyche. "The representatives of all
the forces originating in the interior of the body and transmitted [übertragenen] to the mental apparatus," instincts
are at once the trans-lation (*Über-tragung*) and the re-presentation of an endosomatic tension. Moreover, just as tension was earlier defined, in reference to the psyche, as a
disequilibrium or difference of forces, so this endosomatic
tension implies both an excess that informs corporeal existence and a corporeal resistance to that excess. The difference between them lends its semantic force to the word
"Trieb," clearly stronger than that of the English "instinct,"
closer yet to that of "drive" but corresponding most pre-

---

[26] "Man könnte sich getrauen . . . die *Metaphysik* in *Metapsychologie* um-
setzen" (*Zur Psychologie des Alltagslebens*, in *Gesammelte Werke*, 4:288); "One
could venture . . . to transform *metaphysics* into *metapsychology*" (*The Psycho-
pathology of Everyday Life*, in *Complete Psychological Works*, 6:259).

cisely, as Laplanche and Pontalis suggest,[27] to that of the French "pulsion," given the virtual synonymity of *treiben* and *pousser*; and it leads Freud, in his theory of the instincts, to endow with paradigmatic import an activity whose essential role in Bataille we have already discussed, namely, reproduction.

Like Bataille, Freud focuses on reproduction at its most elementary level, that of unicellular organisms and of the germ cell in multicellular organisms, while assuming that the apparent simplicity of this model in no way detracts from its hermeneutical validity. Having remarked that, in multicellular organisms, the "immortality" of the germ cell depends on "the coalescence with another cell similar to itself and yet differing from it" (*JL* 42/34), he asks a question that may be said to anticipate its own answer: "What is the important event in the development of living substance which is being repeated [wiederholt] in sexual reproduction, or in its fore-runner, the conjugation of two protista?" (*JL* 46/38). The "event" called reproduction would evidently amount to the repetition (*Wiederholung*) of this conjugation or copulation, this confusion or coalescence, and is more pointedly inscribed within the "development of living substance," of which any given cell is but a discontinuous embodiment. Freud will accordingly recognize that "immortality" pertains to the "living substance" and that it spells indeed the very mortality of the discontinuous being: "In this sense protozoa too are mortal; in their case death always coincides with reproduction" (*JL* 50/41). In other words, we encounter here a theoretical insight virtually identical to that which induces Bataille to affirm continuity or death in reproduction as the excess of life itself over discontinuity. Conditioned by this excess, the discontinuous being—the unicellular organism, the germ cell, or the multicellular organism itself, in which the reproductive function has been differentiated and to

---

[27] Jean Laplanche and J.-B. Pontalis, *Vocabulaire de la psychanalyse* (Paris: PUF, 1973), 360.

which therefore, as Bataille observes, a "delay" or "re-prieve" is granted—represents no more nor less than *the differential economy of its own death*. The discontinuous em-bodiment of continuity is the form in which the imper-sonal excess of life differentiates itself; and the repetition of this excess, the death of the discontinuous being, is not a return to inanimation but sooner to "the same differen-tiation which produces and exceeds life."[28] In short, death and life are not opposed, for life is the *différance* (and the repetition) of the mortal excess that informs it, at once the resistance and the surrender to an exteriority always al-ready within. Nor therefore are the death and the life *in-stincts*, in the properly psychoanalytic sense of the term, as the psychic translation and representation of the soma's in-ternal exposure, as the psychic expression of a dissymme-try earlier described as constitutive of binding, in any way opposed: instinctual behavior is aim-inhibited to the extent and only to the extent that the end or goal it pursues is the means to its own deferral, that the *telos* it seeks coincides with the difference that is its *archē*. The *Umwege* or detours to which life recurs in its pursuit of death are not belatedly imposed upon it from without, but constitute the circu-itous *Todeswege* internal to life itself. The correlation be-tween the instincts and the compulsion to repeat need not be sought elsewhere than in life's inability not to defend itself against death by reliving the experience of its own mortality. In the end, the subject of *Jenseits des Lustprinzips* is none other than the *für-sich* or for-itself of this very sub-jection to the Other of intersubjectivity.

Thus, both Freud and Bataille underscore an intersub-jectivity that, at once conditioning and exceeding subjectiv-ity as separation, is functionally analogous to the intersub-jectivity Beckett describes in terms of language or signification. The foregoing excursus was not intended, however, merely to confirm this hypothesis but to provide a broader conceptual framework within which to articulate

---

[28] Libertson, *Proximity*, 22.

the salient predicates of Beckettian intersubjectivity and
hence to discuss the intersubjective function *in its thematic
dimension,* to reunite as it were—and under the caveat formulated earlier—the functional and substantial or thematic perspectives whose distinction opened the excursus
itself. I thus recall the introduction to this study, in which
the question of literature was first raised, while anticipating its conclusion, in which that question recurs, by here
proposing as their mediation a commentary centered on
the "hero as artist," or more precisely, on the "subject of
literature" in the trilogy. The approach to this subject has
been facilitated by the reading of Bataille and Freud, on
the one hand because, in accordance with the differential
logic intrinsic to intersubjectivity or intertextuality itself
(and which of course would enable one, as is implicitly the
case here, to read Bataille and Freud, among others,
through Beckett), the same is genuinely understood only
by virtue of the alterity that constitutes it, and on the other,
because the functional affinity of Bataille's and Freud's
work with Beckett's own projects a properly thematic configuration embracing the preoccupations of all three as instances of the *same* economy. One thinks not only of the
fundamental role of myth and dream in Freud, of desire
and death in Bataille, but also and more importantly for
our purposes, of its association with the sustained interest
demonstrated by both in the specifically literary, an interest they obviously share with Beckett and of which the pre-
ceding discussion already suggests at least a summary explanation; for literature, that dimension of language
irreducible to the latter's conception as *technē,* as the mere
means to an end, is clearly of a piece, for Bataille, with
those "sovereign" activities which exceed the world of
work or utility,[29] and as just such an excess may be said to
characterize, in Freud's words, "purely instinctual as con-

[29] See the list cited in n. 8, above, and in which figure "les arts." The
point is more substantially confirmed by a reading of *La Littérature et le
mal,* especially of the response to Sartre concerning signification in
Baudelaire.

trasted with intelligent efforts [ein rein triebhaftes im Ge-
gensatz zu einem intelligenten Streben]" (*JL* 41/33). For
Freud and Bataille no less than for Beckett, literature or
art in general represents one of the most conspicuous effects of a universe in which the human subject, be it individual or collective, discovers that it is *not* alone. It thus
remains to be seen, more thoroughly than heretofore, how
the trilogy as a whole describes, to use Blanchot's expression, the "essential solitude" of a subject inextricably involved with an impersonal alterity.

· · ·

The introductory section of this chapter stated, primarily
in reference to the second part of *Molloy*, the dissymmetrical relation between an intersubjective Other and the
subjectivity it conditions. In the paradigmatic case of
Moran, the conditionality of subjectivity as separation
manifests itself in the hero's belated awakening to his own
pre-originary alterity and in the attendant compulsion,
embodied by a voice neither his own nor that of another
subject, neither inside nor outside—a compulsion incom-
prehensible moreover in terms of the utilitarian world he
formerly inhabited—to (re)write this very self-disposses-
sion. The compulsive character of his (re)writing, in its
fundamental correlation to the alterity and to the repeatability, in a word, to the iterability of the first person, bespeaks a universe in which the Husserlian "einsame Seelenleben," the solitude or separation of a subject free and
able to remain silent, is conditioned and exceeded by the
inability not to speak, in which the silence proper to the first
person can be imposed upon the impersonal voice of intersubjectivity only if the first person ex-presses itself. In the
words of the Unnamable: "The search for the means to
put an end to things, an end to speech, is what enables the
discourse to continue" (*I* 21/299). Reminiscent of expression as it was defined in the introduction to this study, as
well as of Bataillian transgression and the repetition com-

pulsion in Freud, iter-ability—at once the alterability and the repeatability of the Beckettian subject—is not an "ability," a "possibility" or power, but an impossibility and a necessity, or, as Beckett would have it, an "obligation." In Moran's case no less than in that of his successors, albeit ever more explicitly as the trilogy progresses, this necessity and this impossibility, to the very extent that they inform the dispossession of that silence proper to the first person, may be said to characterize the quest for an answer to the question of who is speaking. And just as the imposition of silence entails a renewal of its dispossession, so every answer to this question—Moran, Molloy, Malone, the Unnamable—merely succeeds in reopening the question itself. The aim-inhibited nature of the quest that *is* the trilogy attests, as we shall see, to the paradox of an equivocal intersubjectivity whose relation to subjectivity as separation is itself uni-vocal: the compulsion to reopen the quest(ion) of subjectivity yields a repetition of the intersubjective confusion wherein that very compulsion originates. And it is precisely the univocity of this relation—what was called, in the first chapter, the irreversibility of dispossession, and in reference to Freud and Bataille, life as the *différance* of death—that enables one to read the quest(ion) of subjectivity as a narrative.

As the first chapter suggested, however, the progression of the trilogy as a narrative is, paradoxically, regressive, insofar as its fundamental irreversibility or univocity pertains to a temporality that dispossesses historical time itself. What this means is that each repetition of the difference that is (inter)subjectivity raises that difference to yet another power, that the impossibility and the necessity of the quest(ion) of subjectivity become ever more pronounced, as does of course the "impoverishment" of storytelling. I refer not only to the basic elements of plot and setting but, in the present context, to that of character; and it is not merely a matter of acknowledging the increasing reduction of "propriété(s)" to which Beckett's characters, most notably those who are also narrators, find themselves subjected (and which is accompanied, in Molloy and Malone, by the increasingly urgent and forever unfulfilled desire to draw up the inventory of their goods and possessions), but, more importantly, of recognizing that this very reduction assigns an ever more prominent role to an intersubjectivity irreducible to any notion of character. So Molloy, for whom his own mother figures the more advanced dispossession he himself figures for Moran, alludes to imperatives whose source is nowhere identified with a character analogous to Youdi:[30]

> It is true they nearly all bore on the same question, that of my relations with my mother, and on the importance of bringing as soon as possible some light to bear on these and even on the kind of light that should be brought to bear and the most effective means of doing so. Yes, these imperatives were quite explicit and even detailed until, having set me in motion at last, they began to falter, then went silent, leaving me there like a fool who neither knows where he is going nor why he is going there. (*M* 143/86–87)

Bereft of a third person or character who might constitute the pseudocouple Molloy–his mother, the first part of this novel does nevertheless recall or foretell the second regarding the problematic nature of the imperatives by which the protagonist is enthralled. Just as Moran's failure apparently results from his inability to remember the purpose of his mission, so Molloy, having resolved to visit his mother, finds himself, in spite of his explicit and detailed "instructions," resembling "un con qui ne sait ni où il va ni pour quel motif." On the other hand, the absence of a figure analogous to Youdi, who in the second part of the novel sustains the illusion that the *telos* of Moran's mission

[30] On the other hand, Molloy does appear to write at the behest of an anonymous emissary resembling Gaber. That this character appears exclusively within the economy of the *récit*, rather than that of the *histoire*, indicates that the thematic focus of the trilogy has shifted further from the latter to the former and that, yet more clearly than in the case of Moran, this story allegorizes the dispossession of its teller.

may have to do with a character named Molloy, yet more clearly emphasizes, in the first part, the irreducibility of the end of Molloy's own journey to another character:

> And of myself, all my life, I think I had been going to my mother, with the purpose of establishing our relations on a less precarious footing. And when I was with her, and I often succeeded, I left her without having done anything. And when I was no longer with her I was again on my way to her, hoping to do better the next time. And when I appeared to give up and to busy myself with something else, or with nothing at all any more, in reality I was hatching my plans and seeking the way to her house. (*M* 144–45/87)

Considered as a character, Molloy's mother is plainly the pretext of a *recherche* whose eternal incompletion bespeaks the essential excess of intersubjectivity over the separation of same and other. If nonetheless, as I earlier claimed, she may also be said to figure birth and death as the *archē* and the *telos* of Molloy's failure, this is so only to the extent that she represents for him the intersubjective confusion he himself represents for Moran. In fact, both of the passages cited above emphasize, as the origin and the end of Molloy's quest, his "rapports" with his mother, that is, a "space between" corresponding to the equi-vocity that univocally invests and dispossesses the very effort to appropriate it. So again does the greater dispossession or impoverishment of the first relative to the second part of *Molloy*, examples of which were first offered in another context, announce itself not only in spatial and temporal terms—in the aggravated errancy and incompletion of Molloy's story—or simply in the reduction of "propriété(s)" pertaining to its characters, but also in the greater degree to which it focuses on an intersubjective Other irreducible to another or a third subject. In itself, this would of course amount to a rather banal observation, were it not that the inability (not) to name this intersubjectivity is the impossibility of (not) telling this story, and that the paradoxical movement from

the second to the first part of *Molloy* describes a trajectory
according to which each narrator has, more than his predecessor, literally nothing to say.

As the narrator of *Watt* observes, however, "the only way
one can speak of nothing is to speak of it as though it were
something."[31] What this work defines as "the being of
nothing," as "a thing that was nothing," as "that presence
of what did not exist, that presence without, that presence
within, that presence between,"[32] may be said to correspond to the "nothing" of intersubjectivity itself, which is
not to be identified with the *néant* of separation but rather,
as the trilogy no less than *Watt* suggests, with the "as
though" or allegorical character of the Beckettian subject
in its excess over the alternatives of nothingness and being,
and which informs the Unnamable's reflections on how to
name itself: "What am I to do, what shall I do, what should
I do, in my situation, how proceed? By aporia pure and
simple? Or by affirmations and negations invalidated as uttered, or sooner or later?" (*I* 7–8/291). The aporetic situation of the Unnamable, in which the impossibility and the
necessity of naming—of stating, in the language of separation, the Other of separation, of identifying the alterity
of identity—are most apparent, and the telling of stories
most explicitly the allegorization of telling itself, is nevertheless foretold from the very beginning of the trajectory
to which I have just alluded. In reference to his own narrative activity, Molloy pointedly remarks:

> And every time I say, I said this, or I said that, or speak of a
> voice saying, far away inside me, Molloy, and then a fine
> phrase more or less clear and simple, or find myself com-
> pelled to attribute to others intelligible words, or hear my
> own voice uttering to others more or less articulate sounds,
> I am merely complying with the convention that demands
> you either lie or hold your peace. (*M* 145/88)

[31] *Watt*, 77.
[32] Ibid., 39, 76, 45.

The "lie" to which he is condemned—and which, we might note in passing, functions metadiscursively as well, as in the paradigmatic paradox of the liar[33]—not only describes the narrative convention whereby the impersonal voice of intersubjectivity is ascribed to a purportedly self-identical speaker but clearly extends to the very thematization of intersubjectivity *as a voice* ("a voice . . . far away inside me"); and while this thematization will in fact persist, through *Malone Dies* and *The Unnamable*, as a privileged representation and translation of the univocal relation between intersubjectivity and the individual subject, the functional equivocity or confusion of intersubjectivity itself necessarily spawns a plurality of common names or nouns, one of which Molloy proposes in an addendum to the passage quoted above: "En fait je ne me disais rien du tout, mais j'entendais *une rumeur, quelque chose de changé dans le silence*" (*M* 145/88, my emphasis). What is notably translated as "*a murmur, something gone wrong with the silence*," thus takes its place among those designations whose very multiplicity is emblematic of the "noise" each supposedly represents: "that rumor rising at birth and even earlier, What shall I do? What shall I do? now low, a murmur, now precise as the headwaiter's And to follow? and often rising to a scream" (*M* 12/10), "a murmur [that] is born in the silent world" (*MM* 172/277), "these groans that choke me" (*I* 81/335), "this gnawing of termites" (*I* 87–88/339), "the buzzing of an insect" (*M* 81/50), "one vast continuous buzzing"

---

[33] I refer to Epimenides' attribution to the Cretan of the statement that all Cretans are liars. In the trilogy, one of the more memorable instances of this paradox is to be found in the concluding lines of *Molloy*, to which I have repeatedly drawn attention: "Then I went back into the house and wrote, It is midnight. The rain is beating on the windows. It was not midnight. It was not raining" (*M* 293/176). Of course, this paradox, in which the meaning of the *énoncé* calls into question the subject of its own *énonciation*, attains its greatest frequency in *The Unnamable*. It is to be noted, moreover, that the suspension induced by aporia is momentary, for it opens the discourse of truth to a metadiscursive denial that, since it claims for itself the very truth it denies, leads in turn only further into a discursive abyss.

(*MM* 54/207), "countless pantings" (*MM* 53/206), "long silent screams" (*M* 133/81), "that noise you hear when you
really listen, when all seems hushed" (*M* 79/49), "the faint
sound of aerial surf that is my silence" (*MM* 78/221), "a
noise of rushing water, phenomenon mutatis mutandis
perhaps analogous to that of the mirage, in the desert"
(*MM* 182–83/283), "this sound that will never stop" (*I* 103/
349), "that far whisper" (*M* 64/40), "this innumerable babble, like a multitude whispering" (*MM* 168/274), "the ter-
ror-stricken babble of the condemned to silence" (*I* 113/
354), "the comparative silence of my last abode" (*M* 91/56),
"that silence of which, knowing what I know, I shall merely
say that there is nothing, how shall I merely say, nothing
negative about it" (*MM* 78/221), "[the] silence [that] once
broken will never again be whole" (*I* 132/366)—to cite, indeed, but a few. All of these terms essentially refer to an
intersubjective "static," to a heteroglossia[34] or equivocity
that univocally conditions and exceeds the silence of subjectivity as separation. It is this same correlation, between
the univocal and the equivocal dimensions of intersubjectivity, that the Unnamable describes in speaking of a
"voice" at once plural and singular (whose singularity does
not appear, however—any more than that of the "Il,"
"On," "Personne," or "Quelqu'un" in Blanchot—to render
it less equivocal): "But often they all speak at once, they all
say simultaneously the same thing exactly, but so perfectly
together that one would take it for a single voice" (*I* 116/
356). Moreover, this "ils" or "il," in its irreducibility to the

---

[34] As it is used here, the term "heteroglossia" is not unrelated to its
Bakhtinian understanding (see M. M. Bakhtin, *The Dialogic Imagination*,
trans. Caryl Emerson and Michael Holquist, ed. Michael Holquist [Aus-
tin: University of Texas Press, 1981], 263; "heteroglossia" is Emerson's
and Holquist's translation of *raznorečie*). Concerning the trilogy, it is less
instructive as a designation of the coexistence of different types of discourse than as a designation of the effect of that coexistence, that is, the
static of intersubjectivity. Of equal if not greater pertinence are Bakhtin's
statements regarding the novel as a genre or rather a nongenre: as the
exigency of its own failure, the novel is formally as well as historically
suited to subjectivity as separation.

third person understood, as in Derrida's critique of Husserl, to represent the universality or sameness of a subject bereft of any particularity or difference,[35] is what conditions the asymptotic evolution of the trilogy's narrators: while each narrator receives a proper name more belatedly than his predecessor[36] and the role played by an anonymous "I" becomes ever more prominent, the univocal movement of dispossession characteristic of the trilogy as a whole defines an "itinerary" whose terminus remains, precisely, a vanishing one. In other words, dispossession is not negation, and the very effort to silence the static of intersubjectivity merely renews the failure of the first person to coincide with itself in the ideality of the third. That this is so—that the "il(s)" escapes as it approaches, that the first person approximates its self through the incremental loss of that presence (of the "here" and the "now") proper to it, or as the deferral of its own death—all of this implies once again that the univocal intersubjective conditionality of the Beckettian subject will produce an equivocal voice both compelled and unable (not) to name itself and irre-

[35] As I point out in the introduction (see above, pp. 24–27), the sameness of meaning can only be preserved, in the case of the expression "I am," if the "I" itself—which is both the subject and the object of the expression and susceptible, by definition, to change—is reduced. In other words (and paradoxically), the meaning of this expression can only remain the same if "I am" becomes "it is." Derrida remarks, concerning this third "person": *"The present indicative of the verb 'to be' is the pure and teleological form of expression insofar as it is logical—or, better, we should say the present indicative of the verb 'to be' in the third person.* Better still, the pure, teleological form is a proposition of the type 'S is p,' in which S is not a person that one could replace by a personal pronoun, the latter having in all real speech a merely indicative value" (*VP* 81/73). For the purposes of this study, it is absolutely essential to distinguish between the third person as *the* form of objective ideality and the third person as the embodiment of intersubjective impersonality in the general economy—between the "it is" of Husserl, on the one hand, and the "il y a" or "illéité" of Lévinas, the "Il" of Blanchot, the "they" or "it" of Beckett, on the other.

[36] In the French original, Malone, p. 79; Molloy, p. 34; Moran, p. 153 (the first page of his narrative).

ducible to the tautology, to the *logos* of sameness or silence intrinsic to subjectivity as separation. This irreducibility explains in turn why the trilogy in its entirety may be regarded as a "self"-quotation; indeed, the fundamental iterability of the Beckettian subject is the compulsion to speak a language not its own, nor, as we have seen, that of another subject, to speak the "impropriété" of language itself and so to place in quotation the very notion of its "authority."

Perhaps nowhere in the trilogy does the question of authority or authorship arise in more striking a manner than at the beginning of *Malone Dies*, where the narrator speaks of his present situation in a passage that resembles in fact an impoverished quotation of *Molloy* and prefigures its own yet more impoverished quotation by the narrator of *The Unnamable*:

> I am in my mother's room. It's I who live there now. I don't know how I got there. Perhaps in an ambulance, certainly a vehicle of some kind. . . . In any case I have her room. I sleep in her bed. I piss and shit in her pot. I have taken her place. I must resemble her more and more. (*M* 7–8/7)

> Present state. This room seems to be mine. I can find no other explanation to my being left in it. . . . Perhaps I came in for the room on the death of whoever was in it before me. . . . It is not a room in a hospital, or in a madhouse, I can feel that. . . . No, this is just a plain private room apparently, in what appears to be a plain ordinary house. I do not remember how I got here. In an ambulance perhaps, a vehicle of some kind certainly. One day I found myself here, in the bed. (*MM* 13–14/182–83)

> Where now? Who now? When now? Unquestioning. I, say I. Unbelieving. . . . Can it be that one day, off it goes on, that one day I simply stayed in, in where, instead of going out, in the old way, out to spend day and night as far away as possible, it wasn't far. Perhaps that is how it began. . . .

... the place may well be vast, as it may well measure twelve feet in diameter. It comes to the same thing, as far as discerning its limits is concerned. I like to think I occupy the centre, but nothing is less certain. In a sense I would be better off at the circumference, since my eyes are always fixed in the same direction. But I am certainly not at the circumference. (*I* 7, 13/291, 295)

The question of authorship, raised here by an intersubjectivity irreducible to any and all three narrators and that may indeed be defined as their very difference, is also the question earlier characterized as central to the trilogy and posed by Blanchot at the outset of his own meditation of that work, namely: "Who is speaking in Samuel Beckett's novels?" Although, as I have noted, this question cannot be exhausted by any answer, it inevitably produces a response that Blanchot himself cites: "By a reassuring convention, we answer: it's Samuel Beckett."[37] Prejudice alone would lead us to believe that this convention has been or even could be dismissed once and for all from the critical study of literature, and hence that it need not be examined anew whenever it is invoked. In a very definite sense, the perennial invocation of an authorial agency grounded in separation may be considered the form in which the eternal return of the question of (inter)subjectivity dissimulates itself. Thus does Blanchot reopen the question:

> Who is speaking here? Is it "the author"? But what can this word designate, if in any case he who writes is no longer Beckett, but the exigency that has carried him outside of himself [hors de soi], dispossessed him, abandoned him to the outside [l'a livré au dehors], making of him a being without a name, the Unnamable, a being without being who can neither live nor die, neither cease nor begin, the empty place wherein speaks the idleness of an empty speech and which is more or less concealed by a porous and agonizing "I."[38]

[37] *Le Livre à venir*, 289.
[38] Ibid., 290.

Blanchot's "answer" might be reformulated as follows: if the voice of the trilogy is to be construed as the allegorical self-representation of its author, the essential non-self-co-incidence of the former defines the latter as already an allegory. In still other words, one may say here that the relation between author and narrator is analogous to the relation between narrator and character: we have seen, through a reading of the second part of *Molloy* whose fundamental claims are applicable to the trilogy as a whole, that and how the story of a character's dispossession thematizes the impossibility of properly thematizing its narrator's non-self-coincidence; and in moving from narrator to author, we do not enter an extratextual world in which this non-self-identity would prove to be merely the aesthetic alteration of a self-identical subject but rather find ourselves in an intertextual universe where the non-self-coincidental voice of the trilogy thematizes literature itself as the ex-pression of a subjectivity beyond separation. Blanchot's own vocabulary, reminiscent of Freud's and still more of Bataille's—especially such terms as "hors de soi" and "au dehors," in their correlation to an exigency and to an impossibility or powerlessness—underscores the *inter*subjective nature of an authorial function[39] corresponding to the *inter*textuality of the trilogy itself. By examining here the thematization of this function in the ever greater dispossession of the trilogy's narrators, we grasp the necessity of a general reconsideration of literature, including its

---

[39] Although it does not serve even as the implicit subtext of my argument here, Michel Foucault's lecture entitled "Qu'est-ce qu'un auteur?" (*Bulletin de la société française de philosophie*, July–September 1969: 73–95) contains a number of formulations that suggest an affinity between his thought on the subject and the tendency of this argument. The most striking example is one that also recalls Blanchot: "Il serait tout aussi faux de chercher l'auteur du côté de l'écrivain réel que du côté de ce locuteur fictif; la fonction-auteur s'effectue dans la scission même, —dans ce partage et cette distance" (87). On the other hand, it is strange, to say the very least, that, many years after the publication of both *L'Espace littéraire* and *Le Livre à venir*, Foucault should claim that "la théorie de l'oeuvre n'existe pas" (79).

authorship, emphasized in the conclusion to this study. It is already clear, however, from the "quotation" of *Molloy* inaugurating *Malone Dies*, that the "self" of this quotation is precisely the difference of their narrators' sameness, that the sameness of their author is precisely the iterability of an impersonal *Personne*.

While Blanchot, for strategic reasons, clearly privileges *The Unnamable*, we do indeed reach a center of Beckettian intersubjectivity in what is literally the inter-text of the trilogy, that is, in *Malone Dies*. In fact, not the least enigmatic feature of Blanchot's essay consists in its relative devalorization or plain neglect of certain elements of the trilogy that would forcefully confirm its own most basic theses. Such elements include, as I have already suggested, the temporal structure of *Molloy*, which invites a comparison of Beckettian time with Blanchot's understanding, crucial to the essay in question, of repetition in difference, of what he calls "le temps de l'absence de temps";[40] but also, in this context, the ways in which *Malone Dies* articulates Blanchot's distinction, no less crucial to his essay on Beckett and essential as well to the definition of intersubjectivity in both thinkers, between *oeuvre* and *livre*. Described as that of which, from the perspective of what Blanchot himself calls separation, one grasps only "the substitute, the approach and the illusion in the form of a book,"[41] the *oeuvre* may be said to embrace the internal *fêlure* that makes of *Molloy* neither a single nor two books (itself produced, as I have shown, by a *fêlure* internal to each story), as well as the intertextual communication of *Molloy* and *Malone Dies* to which I have just alluded, and the dimension of *Malone Dies* itself that exceeds the stories told by its narrator (not to mention *The Unnamable*, which exceeds, in its turn, the story of Macmann's-Malone's purported death). This dimension is of course not wanting in *Molloy*: that the protagonist of each story should turn out to be the allegorical

---

[40] *L'Espace littéraire*, 26.
[41] Ibid., 16.

representation of its narrator's non-self-identity means that the former's discursiveness or errancy thematizes a functional "écart de langage,"[42] or language *as* a functional *écart* that produces not only its own narrative allegorization but also the discursive supplement or metadiscourse whose focus is precisely narration itself. Nor, to be sure, is the metadiscursive dimension of *Malone Dies* missing from *The Unnamable*, where, much more explicitly than in *Molloy*, the fundamental predicates of a subjectivity beyond separation ascribed to a character or characters (in this case, Mahood and Worm) are held to pertain, first of all, to the narrator. The specificity of *Malone Dies* thus resides, not in its being conditioned by the general economy of the *oeuvre*, since this is true of all three books, but rather, as the "place" it assumes in the temporality of the trilogy already suggests,[43] in its (metadiscursive) description of the subjective experience of that economy. For just as this book may be said to occupy, within the trilogy as a whole, a moment at which the communication of past and future yields a present that does not pass, a moment in which nothing occurs or sooner recurs, "an instant without bounds" (*MM* 97/233) where, in Blanchot's words, "règne l'indécision du recommencement,"[44] in short, a dead time (already operative, as we have seen, in *Molloy*, albeit less conspicuously) wherein the infinite contraction of time itself and the infinite dilation of the instant embody the approach of death as its asymptotic deferral—so the description of Malone's experience distinguishes itself from that of Moran's, Molloy's, and the Unnamable's by the *relatively* greater emphasis it places on indecision and especially on inaction or *désoeuvrement*. The equivocity underlying both this inaction and this indecision is only ostensibly eluded, and in fact will become more pronounced, by virtue of Malone's initial decision to adopt a strategy that would make of writing a

[42] Moran states: "Il me semblait que tout langage est un écart de langage" (*M* 193/116).
[43] See chap. 1, above, n. 31.
[44] *L'Espace littéraire*, 18.

"possible" activity: "While waiting I shall tell myself stories, if I can. They will not be the same kind of stories as hitherto, that is all. . . . Now it is a game, I am going to play" (*MM* 8–9/180). Narration will be a "game" insofar as these stories, in contrast to those told hitherto (in *Molloy*), will not purport to tell the truth, only to show, by their failure, that truth is the repetition of an error, but will define themselves from the very outset as pure fiction. To be more precise: rather than to speak, as do both Moran and Molloy, of a homonymous character as though he were the same as the narrator, and hence to embrace once again the discourse of a subject unable to state its own sameness except through the allegorization of its non-self-identity, Malone will speak of a character, first named Saposcat and subsequently Macmann, as though he were another, and thereby assume a language for which, since its *telos*, like that of a game, remains entirely internal to it, the question of a failure akin to Molloy's or Moran's presumably cannot arise, and the avowal of whose fictional status would appear moreover to lend an added credibility to the narrator's metadiscursive commentary concerning his own situation. And it is this apparent separation of languages, designed to elude the equivocal *écart* of allegorical discourse and reflected even in the typographical structure of the novel, that explains in return the uncharacteristic decisiveness of these early pages, especially of a statement such as: "This time I know where I am going . . . " (*MM* 9/180).

As its formulation here implies, however, Malone's approach to writing is at best but the reverse of Moran's or Molloy's, and no less prone to failure or error since, like theirs, it assumes an economy of separation that is itself ungrounded in the equivocity of the "as though." So it is that, only shortly after having begun the sluggish story of Sapo, the narrator interrupts himself to remark: "What tedium. And I call that playing. I wonder if I am not talking yet again about myself. Shall I be incapable, to the end, of lying on any other subject?" (*MM* 23/189).[45] While it seems that this question might be characterized as merely rhetorical in the sense that, implicitly denying the very necessity of its being asked, it would presuppose a decisive answer (in the case at hand, evidently an affirmative one), it must be pointed out that the "autre chose" ("other subject") to which it refers invokes a more fundamental indecision regarding the relation between self and other. In other words, the question of Malone's inability to lie "on any other subject," of his inability to speak of another as though he were self-identical and hence, ultimately, to tell stories, correlative to the question of an inability *not* to lie about himself, of an inability not to speak of his self as though it were another, to tell stories and inevitably to fail as a storyteller, is itself and can only be opened by the undecided or undecidable ontological status of this speaking subject. The question: About whom does the narrator lie?, which already underscores the ineluctability of lying, of the "as though," then becomes: Who is the narrator?; and to say that the narrator *is this question* is to define the subject of this novel as an equivocal intersubjective relation that conditions and exceeds the separation of self or same and other. Thus, the supposed separation of languages— of a story or stories told in the third person, on the one hand, and on the other, a first-person metanarrative— which is mirrored, again, in the very typography of *Malone Dies*, turns out to be the *béance* of subjectivity as a quest(ion), a *fêlure* or *écart* within which the movement of the novel resembles nothing so much as an endlessly indecisive "va-et-vient" between the ontological alternatives enunciated by Malone himself in the formula: "[to] be another, *in myself, in another* [être autrui, *en moi, en autrui*]" (*MM* 34/195, my emphasis). That the dimension of this errancy or dis-course does in fact exceed the stories it also

[45] In the French original, the third sentence runs as follows: "Je me demande si ce n'est pas encore de moi qu'il s'agit, malgré mes précautions."

and at once conditions identifies it, furthermore, as the locus or space not only of Malone's essential indecision, but
also, as I earlier suggested, of his no less essential inaction
or *désoeuvrement*: the abandonment of his original program
("Present state, three stories, inventory, there" [*MM* 12/
182]), the fragmentation and incompletion[46] of the only
remaining story or stories (that, or those, of Sapo and Macmann), the boredom and fatigue, the anxiety and disgust,
the impotence so often voiced by Malone in reference to
writing, to this pastime in which time fails to pass—all con-
tribute to the description of subjective experience in an
economy where the separation from or negation of being
upon which are predicated both work or action and the
attendant "accomplishment of the world" does not obtain.
Blanchot's own characteristically paradoxical insistence on
dés-oeuvrement as a salient attribute of subjectivity in the
very economy of the *oeuvre* draws attention to the excess
of this same economy over that, grounded in negation or
separation, that is, in closure, of the *livre*; and this excess,
which does not indicate so much a distinction between *livre*
and *oeuvre* as indeed the irreducibility of the latter to the
former, and in the present case, of *Malone Dies* to its third-
person narratives, clearly corresponds for Blanchot to a
conception of (the being of) subjectivity irreducible to that
which founds what Beckett would call the "feasible" world.
The statements, "What [the work] says is exclusively this,
that it is—and nothing more," and, "Where [the writer] is,
only being speaks—which means that language [la parole]

---

[46] To predicate incompletion of this story may at first seem unjustified,
since it is commonly held to end, like many another, with the death of its
hero (not to mention its narrator). However, it remains strictly impossible
to determine not only when but whether Macmann(-Malone) dies (just as
it is not clear of what, precisely, the end should consist); and to call this a
"central uncertainty" of the novel (John Fletcher, "Malone 'Given birth to
into death,' " in *Twentieth Century Interpretations of "Molloy," "Malone Dies,"
"The Unnamable,"* ed. J. D. O'Hara [Englewood Cliffs, N.J.: Prentice-Hall,
1970], 58), is at best to state the obvious and at worst—as though the task
of the critic were to reduce this uncertainty—to ignore the trilogy's intersubjective or intertextual definition of such terms as "death" and "end."

no longer speaks, but is, consigns itself to the pure passivity of being,"[47] ascribe to the work and to the writer a language that does not efface or negate itself in view of a purportedly non- or extralinguistic *telos*, that does not *work*, but rather and precisely fails to do so, whose *pourquoi* remains indistinguishable from its impersonal *pour-soi*, a language that is itself *désoeuvré* and whose (re)appearance, like that of the broken *Werkzeug* in Heidegger, announces "the being that is at the heart of the absence of being, that is when there is nothing," "what still speaks when all has been said."[48] In its Blanchotian understanding, the language of being or the being of language defines the (being of the) writer or work *as* the failure of negation, as the "residue" of separation, as the outside that both invests and surpasses closure, and so explains why, in Beckett no less than in Blanchot, the *désoeuvrement* intrinsic to the subject of the *oeuvre* is of a piece with the interminability of the *oeuvre* itself. And while this interminability evidently refers us to *The Unnamable* and beyond, it already and fully informs *Malone Dies*: as, so to speak, the inability to be the term of a relation, in an economy where the relation or outside called intertextuality or intersubjectivity impedes the very constitution of terms, so that the narrator deceptively named Malone and the work of which he is supposedly the author might least inaccurately be designated the anonymous "space between" two voices; but also, of course, as the inability to be a terminus, to enact the end. In this respect, it is of no use for the interpretation of the trilogy to consider, as has been done, whether or when Malone dies, since, on the one hand, this present indicative, like the imperfect in Proust, evokes a time that does not pass and in which Malone's death is precisely the experience of a failed negation or separation, and on the other, the proper name Malone only dissimulates an impersonal Other that engendered and will survive the "person" that

[47] *L'Espace littéraire*, 14–15, 21.
[48] Ibid., 26, 20.

name claims to identify. Shortly before his evacuation, the narrator of *Malone Dies*, anticipating that of *The Unnamable*, observes—in the present indicative: "I am being given, if I may venture the expression, birth to into death . . . [Je nais dans la mort, si j'ose dire]" (*MM* 183/283).

It is nevertheless no accident that, despite the aforementioned pertinence of *Malone Dies*, Blanchot's concept of the *oeuvre* figures most prominently in his comments on *The Unnamable*; nor, as we shall see momentarily, is it an accident that this concept receives one of its most concentrated formulations in the section of *L'Espace littéraire* entitled "La Solitude essentielle." I have already alluded to the aporetic situation in which the Unnamable initially and, for that matter, forever finds itself, and which unites the principal predicates of Beckettian (inter)subjective experience emphasized in this chapter. The task of naming, in the language of separation, the Other of separation itself, produces in the narrator of this volume an indecision regarding even the choice of a method by means of which to fail at this task ("By aporia pure and simple? Or by affirmations and negations invalidated as uttered, or sooner or later?"), as well as the *désoeuvrement* Blanchot will be quick to point out. At the same time, it is clear from the first ("I, say I" [*I* 7/291]) to the last lines of the novel ("You must go on, I can't go on, I'll go on" [*I* 213/414]), and more so even than in its predecessors, that this task, often described as a "pensum," has as a corollary of its intrinsic impossibility a relentless compulsion or necessity. And finally, these attributes reflect in turn the experience of an equivocal intersubjectivity whose relation to subjectivity as separation is itself univocal: the (re)birth, beyond Malone's apparent death, of a subject unable not to speak attests to the fundamental dissymmetry between the rumor of an impersonal exteriority and the silence of the Husserlian "einsame Seelenleben." Blanchot's remark: "When writing means giving oneself over to the interminable, the writer who agrees to bear the essence of this experience loses the power to say 'I,' "[49] must not, of course, be held to imply that the Unnamable does not say "I," but rather that this "dire" is not a "pouvoir," that it is in fact the inability not to say "I." However, since this impossibility pertains to a subject that compulsively exceeds itself, the "I" of *The Unnamable* must be understood to designate precisely this excess, the differentiation of an impersonal intersubjectivity, what Blanchot calls "le 'Il' qui se substitue au 'Je' " while dissociating this third "person" from both the freedom (and power) of another subject and, which amounts to the same, the in-difference of objectivity:

> "Il" does not designate objective disinterestedness or creative detachment. "Il" does not glorify consciousness in another, the development of a human life that, in the imaginary space of the work of art, would retain the freedom of saying "I." "Il" is myself become no one, others become the other; it means that, where I am, I can no longer address myself and that he who addresses me does not say "I," is not himself.[50]

As this passage further suggests, the undecidability or, indeed, the unnamability of the authorial or artistic subject corresponds to the spatial indeterminability or "between" of intersubjectivity itself. If, not only in Blanchot but also in the philosophy of difference, the subjective experience of intersubjectivity is associated with a certain outside or exteriority, this is due, as I have indicated elsewhere,[51] to the rhetorical strategy of reversal and reinscription by virtue of which the devalorized term of a separation comes to describe the other of that very separation, and which in this case reverses the priority ascribed by the philosophy of separation to the subject *as* interiority in favor of the intersubjectivity that conditions it. Thus, for subjectivity, the outside and the "between" of its intersubjective condi-

---

[49] Ibid., 21.

[50] Ibid., 23. I leave the word "Il" in French because it can mean either "it" or "he." As Blanchot implies, either sense of the term, taken separately, can lead to misunderstanding.

[51] See introduction, n. 28.

tionality are fundamentally indistinguishable.[52] And this *espacement* or spacing, to whose implicit function in *Malone Dies* I have just brought attention (although, as we have also seen, its effects are explicitly formulated on the thematic level of Malone's own experience), understandably becomes one of the principal foci of the novel whose unnamable subject is virtually confused with intersubjectivity. Whence, to cite but one of many examples, the narrator's self-characterization as "a pure ear" (*I* 112/354), that is, as the difference of a voice whose assumption by the narrator itself only echoes or reiterates its indeterminability, a difference described at greater length yet in similar terms when it is said:

> Perhaps that's what I feel, an outside and an inside and me in the middle, perhaps that's what I am, the thing that divides the world in two, on the one side the outside, on the other the inside, that can be as thin as foil, I'm neither one side nor the other, I'm in the middle, I'm the partition, I've two surfaces and no thickness, perhaps that's what I feel, myself vibrating, I'm the tympanum, on the one hand the mind, on the other the world, I don't belong to either. (*I* 160/383)

Underscored by the recurrent "perhaps," the undecidable identity of this speaker leads it no sooner to adopt than to abandon another pronoun for itself,[53] in a manner no doubt reminiscent of the "methodological" considerations mentioned earlier but that nevertheless brings us closer to

----

[52] To this it must be added, however, that the designation of intersubjectivity as a "space between" may foster the illusion that the intersubjective relation amounts to a reciprocity between two subjects, itself susceptible of being panoramically totalized by a third subject. On this problem in Blanchot, see Libertson, *Proximity*, 279.

[53] At this point (*I* 114/355), in fact, it resumes the narrative of Worm, like Mahood before, a "vice-exister" of "that unthinkable ancestor of whom nothing can be said" (*I* 110/352). Not only Worm and Mahood, but also Malone, Molloy, Moran, and even Mercier and Camier, Watt, and Murphy are considered its "vice-existers"—"my delegates" (*I* 17/297), "my creatures" (*I* 22/300), "my mannikins [mes homuncules]" (*I* 32/306), "my troop of lunatics" (*I* 35/308), etc.

the formulation of a basic affinity between Beckett and Blanchot. Thus: "I shall not say I again, ever again, it's too farcical. I shall put in its place, whenever I hear it, the third person, if I think of it. Anything to please them. It will make no difference. Where I am there is no one but me, who am not [Il n'y a que moi, moi qui ne suis pas, là où je suis]" (*I* 114/355). Not only does this passage imply that both pronouns—"I" and "he"—remain inadequate to the intersubjective *espacement* that exceeds them, to what will subsequently be called "the everlasting third party [l'éternel tiers]" (*I* 147/375); it no less clearly suggests that, in the essentially affirmative dimension of this inadequacy, the dimension of the *oeuvre* "which affirms nothing,"[54] which affirms the nothing(ness) of intersubjective excess, subjectivity *is* the experience of a solitude ("Il n'y a que moi") wherein, by reason of its own non-self-coincidence ("moi qui ne suis pas, là où je suis"), the self or subject is *not* alone. By referring to this solitude, which is thoroughly constitutive of Beckett's *oeuvre*, as "essential" (in contrast to "solitude in the world"),[55] Blanchot does not, in his implicit critique of phenomenology, merely indulge a penchant for the paradoxical but remains faithful to the very paradox on which the phenomenological understanding of the subject is founded. Indeed, as we observed in the introduction, the Husserlian notion of subjectivity as a "solitary mental life" ("einsame Seelenleben") born *ex nihilo* or "in the same instant" ("im selben Augenblick") and whose identity purportedly guarantees its indefinite repetition as such, turns out to be grounded in a pre-originary difference or alterity whose own repetition is the *sine qua non* of identity itself. In yet other words, the separation of time and space, of the *res cogitans* and the *res extensa*, of the subjective and the intersubjective, of silence and language, proves to be predicated upon a failure of separation by virtue of which time becomes a temporalization and space a

[54] See Blanchot, *L'Espace littéraire*, 20.
[55] Ibid., 337–40.

spacing, upon a *fêlure* or, as Blanchot says, "the fissure where the exterior is an intrusion that suffocates . . . where space is the vertigo of spacing,"[56] where thought is a passion and the silence of the subject's solitary life becomes the impersonal rumor of its mortality. It is in fact at this point that the communication of Beckett, Blanchot, Bataille, and Freud appears most incontrovertible; for as the introduction also indicated, to realize the purely *ideal* identity or sameness of the "I am" (and of its "living present" ["lebendige Gegenwart"]) is ideally to require the "reduction," that is, the absence or death of any *real* subject capable of its enunciation—which is to say that, in reality, subjectivity expresses itself according to a univocal or centrifugal movement whose vanishing *telos* is precisely the identity of the "je suis" and the "il est,"[57] as Beckett testifies in one of the more memorable statements of *The Unnamable*, to wit: "Je nous manquerai toujours [we'll always be short of me]" (*I* 87/339). Less misleadingly perhaps than as "je" or "il(s)," the impersonal subject of expression—of literature, of the *oeuvre*—is often designated by both Beckett and Blanchot as "on," as "personne," or indeed as "quelqu'un, si j'ose m'appeler ainsi [someone, if I may so describe myself]" (*I* 148/376). "Quelqu'un est là, où je suis seul"[58] describes the impersonality of a work that engenders and survives its own author(s), "of a cause [travail] which," as the departed Moran well knew, "while having need of us to be accomplished, was in its essence anonymous, and would subsist, haunting the minds of men, when its miserable artisans should be no more" (*M* 191/114–15).

[56] Ibid., 28.

[57] The ideal identity realized, for subjectivity, in the coincidence of the "je suis" and the "il est," that is, in its own death, is conveyed by Walter Benjamin in his meditation on storytelling when he says of the character in a novel "that the 'meaning' of his life is revealed only in his death" ("Der Erzähler," in *Gesammelte Schriften*, 2:456; "The Storyteller," in *Illuminations*, 100–101).

[58] *L'Espace littéraire*, 27.

In conclusion, we might note that the word "travail" is not here endowed with the same semantic value as in Bataille, where its sense essentially coincides with that of *technē*, of the means to an end. This is confirmed not only by Beckett's translation of "travail" as "cause," which may be understood to designate both a cause and an effect, a goal, a purpose, at once an *archē* and a *telos*, but also, of course, by the description of this "work" as one that "would subsist, haunting the minds of men," beyond its own accomplishment, whose end is thus the means to its own excess. Whence, moreover, its very anonymity; for while Moran alludes to this cause in the context of remarks concerning his quest for Molloy, it is explicitly defined as irreducible to that same quest,[59] and, as my earlier reading of the story suggests, can only refer to the impossible task of representing or, in Freud's expression, of "binding" its failure. And since this failure in turn finds its *archē* in the functional non-self-coincidence of discourse, in the *pour-soi* of its difference, the *telos*, the purpose or *pourquoi* of the work in question evidently coincides with the discursive repetition or re-presentation of discourse itself. To assert that Beckett's trilogy thus raises the question of the ends of literature *in general*, and especially for the modern era, entails no more of an anachronism than does the correlative and entirely legitimate claim that literature always already *is* this question. Indeed, it has been demonstrated more than once in the previous pages that the closure responsible for the success of literary representation is predicated upon the anachronistic repetition of its own failure. Nor however is the scope of this observation limited to the context in which it has arisen, namely, that of first-person prose narrative; for on the one hand, the dispossession of the historical time intrinsic to narration recalls the pre-originary, fugitive confusion of the functional and thematic dimensions of writing wherein, to adopt momentar-

---

[59] "For what I was doing I was doing neither for Molloy, who mattered nothing to me, nor for myself, of whom I despaired" (*M* 190–91/114).

ily the instructive but ultimately untenable perspective of Sartre's *Qu'est-ce que la littérature?*, the distinction between the transparency and the opacity of the sign, between prose and poetry, is blurred, while on the other, this confusion also undoes the distinction between the first and the third person, between the effacement of signification in the soliloquy of the subject and its indicative reappearance in intersubjective discourse. If, as the present study maintains, the singular urgency of Beckett's meditation of (inter)subjectivity required abandoning the third in favor of the first person, this is at least in part because the point of view of the third, whose apotheosis may be identified with that of the novel itself in the nineteenth century, has been and is still so often mistaken for the perspective of a greater, indeed an omnipotent and omniscient *person*— and understandably so, for the traditional third-person narrator, like Youdi the voice of ideality itself, of the "il est" or being as presence, remains by definition immune to that dispossession which is the very stuff of the novel.

Paradoxically, therefore, one may say that the truth of the third person can only be told in or by the first, that the subject of literature becomes what it always already is only when the subject of its *énonciation* becomes the subject of its *énoncé*, when the functional dispossession of which the subject of literature is born becomes the thematic focus of literature itself. The "moment" of this becoming cannot be inscribed within traditional literary history since its own differential temporality dispossesses the historicity that such an inscription necessarily presupposes; and in fact, the trilogy itself might well be read as the story of the impossibility of writing a history of the novel. Nor does the truth of this moment amount to that of a revelation, a manifestation, an epiphany, an apocalypse; for as the trilogy amply attests, the thematization of a functional non-self-identity yields at best a negative knowledge, the knowledge of ignorance to which Moran lays claim when he says: "I too was innocent [naïf]. But I knew it" (*M* 232/139), in brief, the knowledge of error as an epistemological undecidability that precedes, founds, and conditions the economy of truth. Hence one of the commoner refrains of the trilogy as a whole, first intoned precisely in reference to the question of whether the impersonal voice of intersubjectivity is properly *understood*, to wit: "La question n'est pas là [That is not what matters]" (*M* 292–93/176). As clearly in Beckett as in Proust, literature is always the question of something else, since its own subject is a quest(ion) that is always elsewhere. And when Blanchot rightly observes that "jamais une oeuvre ne peut se donner pour objet la question qui la porte,"[60] he describes what may be called the "productive paralysis" of Beckett's work, in which it is the very impossibility of stating what (the subject of) literature is that produces literary discourse, while the force of this facilitating impediment increases in accordance with the univocal movement whereby "la littérature va vers elle-même, vers son essence qui est la disparition,"[61] toward the vanishing point at which the sense of literature becomes once again—witness the near-babble of the Unnamable—the transgression or excess of sense wherein it originates. Like its Freudian and Bataillian analogues, this excess signals the problematic closure or end of an era in which the *logos* of subjectivity as separation has proven to be the ineliminable exigency of its own failure. By raising the question of the ends of literature, Beckett may be said to have raised as well that of the ends of humanity, and to have done so, moreover, in his untimely and marginal fashion, at the moment when its discussion was virtually monopolized by a humanist discourse that the trilogy calls radically into question.[62] Yet the intersubjectivity on which this chapter has focused and on whose "reduction" the philosophy of separation is founded, goes by another name whereunder it must be reexamined if we are to gauge the full force of that question which is the Beckettian *oeuvre*, namely, that of error—at once spatial, moral, and epistemological.

[60] *Le Livre à venir*, 273.
[61] Ibid., 265.
[62] The conclusion of the study returns to this subject.

Chapter Three

ERROR

Cette perpétuelle erreur, qui est précisément la "vie."
—Proust

AMONG THE many problems encountered by the reader of Samuel Beckett's trilogy, the problem of space is undoubtedly one of the more complex and formidable. While the present chapter will not venture to provide an exhaustive explication of this problem, one can safely say that the approach to it has by now been quite thoroughly prepared; for as both the introduction and subsequent chapters attest, it is impossible to account for the temporal and intersubjective dispossession of subjectivity as separation without referring to the spatiality on whose phenomenological reduction subjectivity so understood is, after all, explicitly founded. In fact, the terms "temporality," "intersubjectivity," and "spatiality" designate the three principal aspects of a single ungrounding whose problematic nature nevertheless requires precisely that it be considered from a plurality of perspectives. In the Beckettian experience of subjectivity no less than in the critique of the phenomenological theory of language, this ungrounding becomes apparent in a reappearance of the sign whose very secondarity paradoxically testifies to the pre-originarity of an economy in which subjectivity is always already the literal incorporation of intersubjective discourse. The priority of the general economy of signification to the restricted economy of separation entails a reinscription of separation itself, such that time becomes a spacing or *espacement* and space a temporalization, while, for subjectivity, the experience of intersubjectivity takes the form, on the one hand, of a compulsive dispossession of its own historical time, and on the other, of what might be called the equally compulsive exposure to an impersonal dis-course. Moreover, this reinscription of separation problematizes indeed the very terms upon which it operates and in which it necessarily receives its own formulation: as we have seen, the thematization of intersubjectivity as language or discourse is called into question by the function of that same thematization, which may be defined as the signification of a general difference or non-self-identity, including, of course, that of the thematization itself. The alterity constitutive of the sign describes the latter as a figure whose proper sense is always elsewhere; and this not only has led us to replace "literature" within the economy that produces it by examining, as privileged examples, its Bataillian and Freudian analogues, but now suggests that the discourse of Beckett's *oeuvre* should bring us to consider the concept of a general error that, if first defined spatially, is also of a moral or psychological and epistemological nature.[1]

It would be helpful first of all to reiterate the phenomenological reduction as it operates in Husserl's theory of the sign. As we have noted, this reduction paradoxically amounts, within the transcendental sphere, to a bracketing of the sign itself, since the latter, due to its very mediation, precludes the immediate re-presentation of the ideal, pre-expressive object to consciousness. In its rigorously phenomenological sense, speech is privileged over writing precisely to the extent that it is understood *not* to be a sign, to the extent that, in its transparency or self-effacement, it re-presents the signified immediately or "in the same in-

---

[1] As I suggest here, the word "error" is used in this chapter in the three principal senses—spatial, moral, and epistemological—of the verb "to err," the first of which normally assumes the nominal form of "errancy" or "erring" rather than "error." It will further become clear that error is here understood as *prior* and *irreducible* to such distinctions as truth/falsehood and good/evil.

stant" ("im selben Augenblick"), that it preserves the phenomenal interval between subject and object, the identity
of each to itself and hence that presence which is both the
archē and the *telos* of phenomenology. The Derridian critique of this reduction locates its fundamental paradox in
the *archē* that, since it describes the sign as pointless or purposeless (*zwecklos*), would seem to render the reduction itself unnecessary. The originary sameness or identity to self
of the pre-expressive object, that is, the phenomenality
with which it is endowed by subjectivity as separation, is
supposed to constitute the condition of possibility of its
own repetition or re-presentation and would therefore dis-
pense with the mediation of the sign. However, this axiom
is itself undone insofar as the very temporality implied by
repetition remains possible only if the originary instant of
presentation is pre-originarily non-self-identical, only if
the closure of the *Augenblick* is always already opened upon
its own absence.[2] Thus, it is sooner the twin predicates of
signification called difference and repetition that constitute the condition of possibility of identity or sameness;
and the paradoxical reduction of the sign in the phenomenological theory of language proves to be "necessary,"
that is, imperative or compulsive, inasmuch as phenomenology cannot succeed in reaching its *telos* save by repeating the failure or *effondement* of its *archē*. In the present
context, this unfounding indicates not only that the originary and instantaneous presentation of the purportedly
*pre*linguistic object is predicated upon the differential repetition of a signifier that is irreducibly spatial or sensible

[2] It is no doubt significant that Husserl should use the term "Augenblick," which literally means the "blink of an eye," to designate the originary instant of phenomenological *vision*. Insofar as this closure of the eye
corresponds to the phenomenological reduction itself, Derrida's statement, made in reference to the undoing of instantaneity by the temporality of signification, that "there is a duration to the blink, and it closes
the eye" (*VP* 73/65), is misleading. The dispossession of phenomenological vision sooner takes the form, as both Beckett and Blanchot attest, of
an inability to close the eye(s), of an inability not to see.

(either phonic or graphic, since signification is a functional non-self-identity that precedes any such substantial separation or distinction) and hence indicative, but also that presentation or perception in general is already a representation, indeed that the universe of phenomenology is, from its inception, an essentially fictional or *imaginary* universe. To be sure, we must now define the imaginary in a more rigorous fashion in order to grasp the full pertinence of this term to the trilogy. Yet the foregoing remarks clearly suggest the direction to be taken; for if the identity constitutive of perception is ungrounded in the repetition of difference, then the imaginary character of perception itself must be ascribed to the difference of that identity, or, in other words, to the dispossession of that *interval* which is phenomenality. It turns out not unforeseeably that the undoing of the distinction between time and space is at once that of the separation of inside and outside, an undoing that Blanchot describes in elucidating two versions of the imaginary.

"Seeing supposes distance, the decision to be separate, the power not to be in contact and thereby to avoid confusion. Seeing nevertheless means that this separation has become an encounter."[3] According to what Blanchot simply calls "l'analyse commune," imagination would in turn "suppose" perception, where perception is understood, as in the statement just quoted, to suppose separation or negation. Thus: "According to the prevailing view [l'analyse commune], the image is after the object. It is its aftermath: we see, then we imagine. After the object comes the image. 'After' seems to indicate a relation of subordination" (*EL* 32n). However, as he will observe in reference to this reversal of the relation between image and object in a classical aesthetic, its subordination to a universe founded on negation lends to the imaginary the very power correlative to this foundation:

[3] *L'Espace littéraire*, 28. All further references to this work will be given in the text, preceded by the initials *EL*. English translations are my own.

Classical art, at least in its theory, also implied [this reversal], staking its glory on the relating of a likeness to its figure and of the image to a body, on reincorporating it: the image became the invigorating negation, the ideal work whereby man, capable of negating nature, raises it to a higher meaning, either in order to know it or in order to appreciate and admire it. Thus was art at once ideal and true, faithful to the figure and faithful to the truth which is figureless. In the end, impersonality verified works of art. (*EL* 350)

In this its subordination, the image is endowed with the negative power or efficacy of work as a means to that end which is the idealization of the real. This idealization may in fact be considered a kind of phenomenological reduction insofar as, by affirming the resemblance or sameness to self of the object in its imaginary form, it "reduces" the real or empirical non-self-coincidence of the object itself. The "impersonality" to which Blanchot alludes is indeed none other than that of ideality, which in these pages has most often been associated with the "il est" in its superiority to the "je suis."[4] Nevertheless, the aporia discovered in the reduction of subjective non-self-coincidence surfaces as well in the idealization supposedly performed by this version of the imaginary: for just as subjectivity cannot in reality approach its own idealization in the "il est" save by repeating its very *différance* in the "je suis," so the "perceived" object can become itself only through the imaginary re-presentation or re-semblance of its own alterity. It is clearly because, like phenomenology, "l'analyse commune" misleadingly *pre*supposes the *telos* of separation, that Blanchot characterizes its misunderstanding of the relation between image and object as a reversal. Recalling the economy that both conditions and exceeds the universe of separation, the reversal of this reversal is necessarily dissymmetrical and therefore does not preserve the distinction between object and image, perception and imagination:

4 See p. 104, above, n. 35.

After the object would come the image. "After" means that
the thing must first move away in order to be grasped again.
But this distancing [éloignement] is not the simple change of
place of a moving object that would nevertheless remain the
same. Distancing is here at the very heart of the thing. The
thing was there, the thing that we grasped in the living
movement of an act of comprehension—and, transformed
into an image, it instantaneously becomes the ungraspable,
the inactual, the impassive, not the same thing at a distance,
but that thing as distancing, present in its absence, graspable
because ungraspable, appearing as the disappeared, the return of that which does not come back, the strange heart of
distance [lointain] as the life and the sole heart of the thing.
(*EL* 343)

That the thing as image is "le retour de ce qui ne revient
pas" means that what returns is not an originary identity
but a pre-originary semblance, and that the image is not
the copy of an original but instead reveals the thing itself
to have been a re-semblance, "a resemblance that has nothing to resemble" (*EL* 350). Moreover, as Blanchot remarks,
this re-semblance involves an "éloignement" irreducible to
separation: "present in its absence, appearing as the disappeared," the image is a spacing that dispossesses the
phenomenal interval in which a self-identical object manifests itself to an equally self-identical subject, a distancing
that is also an approach or proximity, an escape that is at
once an inescapable "*contact* à distance" (*EL* 28). So it is
that, for subjectivity, the imaginary is experienced as an
"extase" (*EL* 352), as the exposure to an outside already
within and in which the illusory reduction of the imaginary
itself conditioning the power of perception, "the power
not to be in contact and thereby to avoid confusion," gives
way to a "vision that is no longer the possibility of seeing,
but the impossibility of not seeing," in a word, as "fascination . . . the look of solitude" (*EL* 29).[5] As the vision of es-

---

[5] It would be interesting, for many reasons, to compare Blanchot's with
Sartre's version of the imaginary. To some extent, Sartre's own version

sential solitude, "fascination is fundamentally linked to a
neutral, impersonal presence, the undetermined They
[On], the immense, figureless Someone" (*EL* 30), and
would imply that the impersonality earlier ascribed to a
certain aesthetic ideality must in fact pertain, as Blanchot
suggests, to the space in which, due to its own indetermi-
nation, the image lends itself to a mistaken identity: "But
impersonality was also the troubling meeting place where
the noble ideal, concerned with values, and the anonymous, blind, and impersonal resemblance were exchanged,
where each presented itself as the other in mutual decep-
tion" (*EL* 350–51).[6]

It is of more than passing interest to note, finally, the
analogy between these two versions of the imaginary and

may be assimilated to the "analyse commune" of which Blanchot speaks,
in fact it is perfectly plausible that Blanchot had Sartre in mind in elabo-
rating a theory that accounts at once for the possibility of a phenomenology of the imagination and for that which such a phenomenology cannot
explain. Although, in *L'Imagination* (1936), a critique of theories of the
image since Descartes, Sartre insists that the image is in no way subordinated to perception, both there and in *L'Imaginaire* (1940), where he formulates his own theory, the imaginary is conceived as a "néantisation du
monde," as a structure grounded in consciousness as negation. No wonder, then, that his explanation of the compulsion and powerlessness experienced by "la conscience imageante," which represents but one component of a more general polemic against Freud and according to which
"la conscience imageante" is *both* a "croyance" or belief lacking the distance constitutive of power and freedom *and* the non-positional, non-
thetic or pre-reflexive consciousness of itself as such, remains difficult to
accept—unless one denies to pre-reflexive "consciousness" the predicates
that Sartre consistently ascribes it, namely, freedom and power, unless we
see its non-positionality as the dispossession of its separation. What
seems, from a phenomenological point of view, to be a contradiction, appears from a differential perspective as the paradox on which phenomenology itself is founded. This example indicates one direction in which,
beginning with the pre-reflexive *cogito* in its relation to *mauvaise foi* or
more generally to ideology, one might reread the early Sartre.

[6] Blanchot's formulation is potentially misleading, since the apparent
reciprocity implied by the expression "mutuelle duperie" is possible only
if the relation between the space of this exchange or substitution and the
space of ideality, in its separation from the real, is itself nonreciprocal.

the two versions of language to which reference is made in
the question: "In poetry, in literature, is language not, in
relation to ordinary language, what the image is in relation
to the thing?" The analogy is then further developed in a
passage whose pertinence to the trilogy can hardly be ex-
aggerated:

> Does language itself not become, in literature, entirely an
> image, not a language that would contain images or render
> reality in figures but one that would be its own image, an
> image of language—and not a language full of images—or
> else an imaginary language, a language no one speaks, that
> is, a language spoken on the basis of its own absence, as the
> image appears against the absence of the thing, a language
> that is addressed to the shadow of events, not to their reality,
> and by this fact that the words that express them are not
> signs, but images, images of words and words in which
> things become images? (*EL* 31–32n)

By insisting that literary language is *not* "un langage qui
contiendrait des images ou qui mettrait la réalité en figures," "un langage imagé," Blanchot dissociates it at once
from "l'analyse commune" and from "l'art classique," both
of which, as we have seen, subordinate the image to the
reality it idealizes and both of which, by analogy, conceive
literary language as the purely secondary figuration of an
originary linguistic "propriété." This dissociation is no
more arbitrary in the case of language than in that of the
image: just as the thing or object is constituted *as such* only
by its own belated return *as image*, and just as the distinction of the real from the ideal awaits the idealization of the
real itself, so the advent of "le langage courant" (of common, everyday, ordinary, standard language) wherein, as
it is understood here, the self-identical sign effaces itself in
the name of (proper) sense or meaning, is conditioned by
the repetition of the sign as difference, as figure, as semblance, or indeed, as image. The affirmation of a fundamental affinity between image and sign or signification is
not contradicted by their differentiation in the passage

quoted above, since Blanchot therein construes signification or the sign otherwise than does the present study,
namely, as the sign *of* . . . , as the disappearance of language in a world where language serves merely as the vehicle of meaning. This is confirmed by the explicit assimi-
lation of signification and meaning or sense in the
statement: "The image has nothing to do with meaning
[signification], with sense [sens], such as it is implied by the
existence of the world, the striving toward truth, the law
and the light of day" (*EL* 350). At the same time, Blanchot
lends added precision and force to the sense in which I
have spoken of the reappearance of the sign: like that of
the broken tool, the reappearance of the sign signals the
effondement of its own negation and is in this sense imaginary:

> The implement, no longer disappearing in its use, *appears.*
> This appearance of the object is that of resemblance and re-
> flection: if you will, of its double. The category of art is
> linked to this possibility for objects to "appear," that is, to
> abandon themselves to the pure and simple resemblance be-
> hind which there is nothing—but being. Only that which has
> given itself over to the image appears, and all that appears
> is, in this sense, imaginary. (*EL* 347–48)[7]

Any more than that of the broken tool, the (re)appearance
of the sign is *not* a phenomenon but a (re)semblance, since
its "possibility" exceeds negation or separation and does so
precisely to the extent that separation is conditioned by it.
That art is related to this possibility recalls the claim, made
in the introduction, that literature or art in general is possible as the excess of separation only if (the power of) sep-

---

[7] Blanchot's use of the word "object" to designate the tool could evidently lend itself to misunderstanding. Since the object *as phenomenon* appears only with the dis-appearance of the means of its perception, the
appearance of the tool (or the sign), which, again, Blanchot here calls an
"object," is predicated upon the dis-appearance of the object *as phenomenon,* or of phenomenality itself. In other words, the appearance in question is, paradoxically, the undoing of phenomenality.

aration is always already ungrounded in its own "impossibility" or failure; and what this means in the present context is not that literary language properly precedes "le langage courant" but rather that it attests, in its very secondarity, to the origin of the proper in an economy where sense always exceeds itself. "An image of language . . . or else an imaginary language, a language no one speaks," literature reopens the space in which the "sens" of subjectivity is its centrifugal direction and whose impersonality is the confusion of the "je suis" and the "il est," or, in Blanchot's expression, "a relation between here and nowhere" (*EL* 344). The spatial dispossession described by this version of the imaginary may thus be considered an appropriate prolegomenon to the interpretation of error or discourse in the trilogy.

For this interpretation, it is no mere coincidence that the problem of spatial error first arises, in historical terms, at the very moment when historical time itself is dispossessed. As we observed in the first chapter, Moran's story begins with the return of Molloy *as* Moran's own *à venir*, annunciated by Gaber's intrusion into the closure of his "petite propriété," itself implicitly the topological figure of subjectivity as separation. And just as the reversal conditioning the illusory originarity of historical time conditions as well the no less illusory originarity of the distinction between inside and outside, so the reversal of this reversal not only recalls the temporality of difference and repetition whose immemorial past and indefinite future communicate in a paralyzed present, but also and inevitably reopens separation to the inextricable confusion of outside and inside, of the "here" and the "elsewhere,"[8] in which it originates. Nor, as we shall see presently, is it by any means accidental that the space of Moran's subsequent disorientation is precisely that of the senses (or rather of their imaginary dis-

_____

[8] In the interest of terminological clarity, it should be observed that "elsewhere" is here understood as another "here," and "nowhere" as their confusion.

possession), those mediators between the outer and the inner world whose unreliability so confirmed a Cartesian might surely have suspected from the first. The following fragment of Nietzsche's is quoted here, not because it underscores a general correlation between temporal reversal and spatial error (although it also does this) but because, in its critique of the phenomenality of perception, it provides an additional and valuable clue to the reading of error in the trilogy:

> The phenomenalism of the "inner world." The chronological inversion, so that the cause enters consciousness later than the effect.— We have learned that pain is projected to a part of the body without being situated there—we have learned that sense impressions naively supposed to be conditioned by the outer world are, on the contrary, conditioned by the inner world; that we are always unconscious of the real activity of the outer world— The fragment of outer world of which we are conscious is born after an effect from outside has impressed itself upon us, and is subsequently projected as its "cause" ["Ursache"].⁹

While this spatiotemporal inversion is certainly instructive in relation to the trilogy, it is firstly to the "example" chosen by Nietzsche that I would draw attention, namely, that of pain. As Freud has taught us, this is not just one example among others but rather the primordial experience of a differential interiority; and it is indeed Freud himself who provides the most eloquent confirmation of this critique, in a passage of *Jenseits des Lustprinzips* whose similarity to Nietzsche's fragment extends even to the terminological level:

> This state of things produces two definite results. First, the feelings of pleasure and unpleasure (which are an index to

⁹ Friedrich Nietzsche, *Werke in Drei Bänden*, 2d ed., ed. Karl Schlechta (Munich: Hanser Verlag, 1960), 3:804; *The Will to Power*, trans. Walter Kaufmann and R. J. Hollingdale, ed. Walter Kaufmann (New York: Random House, 1967), 265.

what is happening in the interior of the apparatus) predom-
inate over all external stimuli. And secondly, a particular way
[Richtung] is adopted of dealing with any internal excitations
which produce too great an increase of unpleasure: there is
a tendency [Neigung] to treat them as though they were act-
ing, not from the inside, but from the outside, so that it may
be possible to bring the shield against stimuli into operation
as a means of defence against them. This is the origin [Her-
kunft] of *projection*, which is destined to play such a large part
in the causation of pathological processes.[10]

If, albeit less explicitly than Nietzsche, Freud here under-
mines the very notion of cause (*Ursache*), this does not pre-
vent him from suggesting, as does Nietzsche, a definition
of the "origin" (*Herkunft*) of the fiction of causality or projection: projection brings into operation the "shield against
[external] stimuli" (*Reizschutz*), that is, the perceptive component of the system *W-Bw/Pcpt.-Cs.* (*Wahrnehmung-
Bewußtsein*/perception-consciousness), when "too great an
increase of unpleasure" ("allzu große Unlustvermehrung")
is produced from within the organism. In other words,
pain is defined once again as a disequilibrium of forces *internal* to subjectivity, which in its turn could be regarded as
a suffering or subjection, as the *logos* of *pathos* or the "pathology" of this disequilibrium; and pain represents the
"origin" of projection insofar as the force investing the
"mental apparatus," in its differential superiority to the resistance of that apparatus, necessarily projects *itself* toward
the outside of interiority. However, it is the very univocity
of this "way" (*Richtung*) or "tendency" (*Neigung*), turning
subjectivity as it were inside out, that produces its subsequent inversion, whereby the outside internal to subjectivity acts *as though* from without (and Freud says "*als ob . . .
nicht von innen, sondern von außen*"), whereby this purportedly external agency, which is in fact, in Nietzsche's
terms, "born after" ("nachgeboren nach") an internal effect, is belatedly projected ("nachträglich projiziert") as the

[10] *JL* 29/23.

cause of that effect. The entire universe of phenomenology, "which is always phenomenology of perception,"[11] is thus (un)grounded in the fiction of causality. To quote Libertson once again: "The *cogito*, in its entirety, is an 'illusion,' the illusion that the effect may precede, found and condition its cause."[12]

We do not herewith neglect the distinction between thinking and perceiving that Descartes took such pains to draw, since this distinction, established in the moment or instant of the *cogito*, separates transcendental from empirical perception, its ideality from its reality, the perception of the spirit, soul, or mind from that of the senses. It is sooner a question of pointing out that the *cogito*, whose moment arrives only with the belated reduction of its difference, cannot "once and for all" found itself—to say nothing of empirical science—except by repeating *ad infinitum* its instantaneous constitution, and hence that its possibility is also its impossibility. Descartes's solution, Descartes's "way," is well known: the force of that difference which compels the *cogito* to repeat itself is *projected* in the form of a deity or *supercogito* whose power sustains the "continuous creation" of which the *cogito* is incapable. Indeed, the structure of this projection corresponds precisely to that of the first proof of God's existence, according to which "it is . . . impossible that the idea of God which is in us should not have God himself as its cause,"[13] in which, in other words, the effect of an effect is idealistically misinterpreted as the cause of its own cause. Thus, the deity destined to guarantee "once and for all" the certainty of perception *in general* is itself the result of what both Nietzsche and Freud describe as the originary error, of what one might also call the imaginary dispossession, of

---

[11] Derrida, *VP* 117/104.

[12] *Proximity*, 35.

[13] René Descartes, *Oeuvres philosophiques*, ed. F. Alquié (Paris: Garnier, 1967), 2:402; *The Philosophical Works of Descartes*, trans. Elizabeth S. Haldane and G. R. T. Ross (Cambridge: Cambridge University Press, 1911; New York: Dover, 1955), 1:142.

the senses. And the same may be said of Youdi. For even though Youdi finally proves to be less reliable for Moran than God for Descartes, Moran's initial naïveté, progressively dispelled by the failure of his story (which may be read as the story of the failure of Cartesian metaphysics), depends entirely on the belated pre-supposition of this Subject whose absence *hic et nunc*, instead of as the sign of an intersubjective "nowhere," is misinterpreted as the proof of its transcendental veracity. Moran's "way" (*voie*) will coincide with the voice (*voix*) attributed to another and greater Subject and heard *as though from without*. So it is that he unthinkingly lends credence to Gaber's statement, or more precisely, assumes that his failure to retain its *telos* or truth is due to a "mere" error or distraction of the senses, to his having misheard and thus misunderstood, while he persists as well in assuming Youdi's Molloy to be "le vrai" (*M* 192/115), another person distinct from his own, to be sought and to be found. Yet the reference to additional Molloys, including "celui de mes entrailles [he that inhabited me]" (*M* 191/115), and of which it is impossible to know "how far these five Molloys were constant and how far subject to variation" (*M* 192/115), as well as the description earlier quoted in its entirety,[14] portray this "character" as anything but clear and distinct. As the return of an impersonal force that impels or projects Moran "toward the outside," Molloy suggests from the very outset that his space, "the Molloy country" (*M* 222/133), is not that of an "elsewhere" distinct from Moran's "here" or habitation but that of an imaginary confusion always already inhabiting the first person.

Having described the recognizably Irish Molloy country, otherwise known as Ballyba, Moran inconclusively concludes: "That then is a part of what I thought I knew about Ballyba when I left home. I wonder if I was not confusing it with some other place" (*M* 224/135). The "great confusion" to which he succumbs well before his departure may

---

[14] See above, pp. 51–52.

be related, in this context, to the undecidable space of his quest, to the involvement of the Molloy country with "some other place" that the text would entitle one to equate not so much with the Moran country, otherwise known as Shitba, as with Moran's "petite propriété" or even more specifically with his "person." For as I have noted elsewhere, Gaber's arrival disturbs Moran's "repos dominical," the rest or repose of this self-coincidental subject, of the Lord or Master of this diminutive domain, conferring upon him, even while he is still seated, a restlessness that Moran in his turn will bequeath to the trilogy's subsequent heroes:

> And yet the poison was already acting on me, the poison I had just been given. I stirred restlessly in my arm-chair, ran my hands over my face, crossed and uncrossed my legs, and so on. The colour and weight of the world were changing already, soon I would have to admit I was anxious. (*M* 161/96)

As we have also observed, Moran then proceeds to waste or lose the next twelve hours (corresponding, in pages, to one half of the entire narrative) in distraction from his quest if not in quest of distraction, and this for the most part within his own home, where "I did nothing but go to and fro" (*M* 180/108). Telling himself: "There is something in this house tying my hands" (*M* 203/122), he returns to the garden, only to discover that in so doing he has merely enlarged the arena of his incapacity:

> Finding my spirits as low in the garden as in the house, I turned to go in, saying to myself it was one of two things, either my house had nothing to do with the kind of nothingness in the midst of which I stumbled or else the whole of my little property was to blame. To adopt this latter hypothesis was to condone what I had done and, in advance, what I was to do, pending my departure. It brought me a semblance of pardon and a brief moment of factitious freedom. I therefore adopted it. (*M* 204/123)

The particular effect for which Moran claims to have em-
braced this second hypothesis does not appear in any way
to detract from its interpretive superiority to the first, since
the entire first half of his story locates the "elsewhere" of
the Molloy country within the "here" of Moran's "petite
propriété" as a whole. However, the first hypothesis can be
said implicitly to denounce a more fundamental error underlying the second, which, in blaming the whole of Moran's little property, still assumes the very distinction between inside and outside the return of whose dispossession
Gaber has already annunciated. To the extent, moreover,
that Moran's departure is also conditioned by this sedative
assumption, it is bound merely to perpetuate his error;
and in fact, the two parts of the story may well be regarded
as the two modes—as the inside and the outside, as the
"here" and the "elsewhere"—in which the "nowhere" or
"between" of intersubjectivity dissimulates itself. A third
hypothesis, to wit, that "the whole of my little property," in
the proper sense of the term, "had nothing to do with the
kind of nothingness in the midst of which I stumbled," will
emerge only with Moran's own return, when the character
becomes the narrator, the difference between them corresponding *not* to the difference between not knowing this
and knowing it but to the difference between not knowing
it and the knowledge of this very ignorance. For the
reader, this knowledge, although frequently foreshad-
owed, is nowhere more clearly communicated than in the
last lines of the narrative ("It was not midnight. It was not
raining"), which, in their denial of the first, do not affirm
a sense other than the proper sense of Moran's story but
leave the reader no less than Moran himself temporarily
suspended in the undecidable ambiguity of its dispossession. Insofar as this dispossession amounts to a reappearance of the sign as that which is no longer subordinated to
but sooner conditions its own disappearance, to a textual
re-flection that mirrors the story's own textuality, we can
say that the story has been turned inside out, or rather outside in, since it is the purportedly extralinguistic universe

of the story itself that we find once again "within" the economy of signification conditioning it from the beginning. Moran's "petite propriété" is indeed a topological figure, yet the "person" it figures turns out, itself, to be the indeterminable *topos* of its own "impropriété," otherwise known as the Molloy country, the *espacement* or moving space of "a resemblance that has nothing to resemble" for the simple reason that Molloy, instead of another person, is the impersonal prophet of a re-semblance at whose sight the good Father Ambrose, as though fascinated, exclaims: "Is it possible!" (*M* 291/175). It is at this point as well that Moran reinvokes the voice of which he earlier asserted: "And the voice I listen to needs no Gaber to make itself heard. For it is within me and exhorts me to continue to the end the faithful servant I have always been" (*M* 219/ 131–32). As I have suggested, this double inversion, this reversal of the reversal by virtue of which the outside internal to subjectivity, projecting itself toward the outside of interiority, acts as though from without, is itself essentially dissymmetrical and hence does not preserve the illusory distinction between inside and outside born of that projection: if the voice in question is heard from within Moran, it is nevertheless not his own and, in its spatial indeterminability, not only defines this hearing as hallucination but more generally describes the "sens" of subjectivity—its senses, its meaning, and its orientation—as an internal exposure or *ekstasis*, as that distraction or "being-away" which is the being of the imaginary. Henceforth, Moran's way, and that of Molloy, Malone, and the Unnamable, will coincide with this fundamentally non-self-coincidental voice, the superiority of whose force to their own resistance or silence univocally compels each to express itself, to re-flect or re-sound the equivocity or confusion by which they are all engendered. And like Moran's, their homecoming will prove to have been but a long detour or, as Freud would put it, an *Umweg*,[15] since the only home to

---

[15] The decentered circularity implied by the word "Umweg" is evoked

which they can return is precisely the discursive *Unheim-lichkeit* or *errance* that first sent them on their way.

As the earlier reading of Freud would further suggest, the compulsive nature of expression may be associated with the effort to "bind"—to translate and to represent—the failure of binding itself, that is, the inability of subjectivity to contain or restrict the force of intersubjectivity otherwise than through its differential repetition, or, in the terms of the passage just quoted, to shield itself against internal excess otherwise than through a belated projection whereby this excess acts as though from without. Thus, it is precisely the failure of representation that conditions and produces the representation of failure, which is also the illusory or imaginary projection, translation, or transposition of intersubjective discourse into a purportedly extradiscursive universe. To this it must be added, on the one hand, that the intersubjective conditionality of subjectivity renders its own story at once multiple and incomplete and the telling of stories therefore interminable, and on the other, that the force of the discursive compulsion produced by this same dissymmetry increases in accordance with the force of a discursive impossibility. On one level, then, that of the representation of failure, the correlation of this impossibility and this compulsion is indeed represented by a dis-course in what one might call the proper sense of the word, namely, an erring or "running back and forth": from Moran, whose "day of rest" is no sooner disturbed by the order "to see about Molloy"

---

by Molloy, who notes that "having heard . . . that when a man in a forest thinks he is going forward in a straight line, in reality he is going in a circle, I did my best to go in a circle, hoping in this way to go in a straight line" (*M* 141/85), and who ends up describing "if not a circle, at least a great polygon" (*M* 150/90) that lands him squarely in a ditch. The Unnamable remarks: "And my course is not helicoidal . . . but a succession of irregular loops . . . invariably unpredictable in direction, that is to say determined by the panic of the moment" (*I* 66–67/327); but earlier it makes clear the "proper" sense of its discourse when, laboring under the compulsion to speak, it states that "it's round that I must revolve" (*I* 34/307).

than he suffers in the knee "an acute pain" (*M* 198/119) bound to worsen; through Molloy, whose ceaseless search for his mother, hindered by one stiff and one stiffening leg, is eventually pursued through crawling and rolling; and Malone, the genesis of whose own yet greater impotence is described by the degeneration of the able if errant Sapo into the bedridden Macmann; to the Unnamable, the frenzied but no less endless approach to whose disembodiment is embodied first by a head, stuck in a jar, named Mahood, and subsequently by the embryonic or larval Worm, the obligation to move and the inability to do so intensify strictly in concert. Reminiscent of an ambivalence commonly experienced in dreams, this correlation which, due to its very ambivalence, may be predicated as well of the compulsion and the inability to rest, is variously formulated by the narrators themselves: by the Unnamable, simply as "ce besoin de s'arrêter, cette impossibilité de s'arrêter" (*I* 164/385);[16] by Malone, as a "motionlessness [that] too was a kind of groping" (*MM* 82/224); and by Molloy, as a "progress [that] reduced me to stopping more and more often" (*M* 129/78). In every case, however, this paralyzed mobility or mobile paralysis describes an ambivalence or ambiguity intrinsic to the body, as that which is, literally speaking, the differential embodiment or incorporation of an economy that exceeds it; and the ever more aggravated dispossession of the body, by virtue of which alone the body calls attention to itself and its intersubjective constitution, must here be seen to figure a progressively greater expropriation of the universe in which the "reduction" of the body, its subordination to the mind, soul, or spirit, makes of it a "corps propre," the invisible vehicle of a teleological movement. In fact, as much is clearly implied by the statement of Molloy's just quoted, according to which the means of his progress became its

---

[16] I cite the French because the English translation does not do justice to it. Beckett translates "pourquoi ce besoin de parler, ce besoin de s'arrêter, cette impossibilité de s'arrêter" simply as "the cause of talking and never ceasing."

impediment and which evokes the failure of that Cartesian fantasy ascribed by Malone to Macmann, who imagines himself moving "after the fashion of a great cylinder endowed with the faculties of cognition and volition" (*MM* 120/246).[17] What is nevertheless most significant about Macmann's fantasy is that, in its representation of the body as a mere machine, tool, or vehicle, as a purely insensate or inanimate exteriority animated by a pure spirit, it "reduces" the very means of this imaginary separation, that is, the senses. If, as the remarks concerning Freud and Nietzsche would imply, the body is to be construed as an intersubjective "impropriété" that *produces* its own misrepresentation as a "corps propre," it follows that the dispossession of this misrepresentation would appear in the *means* of its production, and that this reappearance of perception *as* imagination is the failure of the representation of failure. Indeed, it is to this failure that Blanchot refers when he characterizes fascination as an "impossibility become visible [impossibilité qui se fait voir]" or as "our own gaze reflected [notre propre regard en miroir]" (*EL* 29–30), in which perception, appearing to itself, impedes and is distracted from its own movement and becomes the perception *of* this distraction and this impossibility. We are thus confronted with yet another paradox of the trilogy, to wit, that the representation of the failure of the body progresses in accordance with the failure of that representation; and this leads its subject to focus ever more on the dis-course or error of language itself.

When Moran states that "tout langage est un écart de langage" (*M* 193/116), he might be said to allude to the *écart* or non-self-coincidence of that voice whose imaginary or hallucinatory advent foreshadows the increasing sensory dispossession befalling each successive incarnation of Beckettian intersubjectivity. The words Molloy hears are

---

[17] See Hugh Kenner, "The Cartesian Centaur," in Esslin, ed., *Samuel Beckett: A Collection of Critical Essays*, 52–61. Moran also has this fantasy (*M* 254/153).

"as pure sounds, free of all meaning," while those he pronounces "were often to me as the buzzing of an insect,"
and his sight has so suffered that "I misjudged the distance
separating me from the other world, and often I stretched
out my hand for what was far beyond my reach, and often
I knocked against obstacles scarcely visible on the horizon"
(*M* 80–81/50). Malone says of himself that "my sight and
hearing are very bad" (*MM* 19/186), and later explains that
his hearing, like Molloy's vision, fails to distinguish between the inner and the outer world: "For a long time now
I have been hearing things confusedly. . . . The noises of
nature, of mankind and even my own, were all jumbled
together in one and the same unbridled gibberish" (*MM*
54/207). And finally, the Unnamable, who claims at the
outset that "what I see best I see ill" (*I* 17/297) and that it
is not yet "stone deaf" (*I* 14/295), evolves beyond Mahood
and Worm toward the condition in which it has always, in
a sense, already been and in which, as though to stress the
imaginary (un)grounding of sensation, it states that "hearing nothing I am none the less a prey to communications"
(*I* 82/336). The failure of the senses in general, whereby
the distinction between inside and outside, the "here" and
the "there" or "elsewhere," succumbs to the confusion of
the "nowhere," not only explains why the apparent contraction of physical confines is accompanied by the sensation of their dilation—why, in Molloy's case, "the confines
of my room, of my bed, of my body, are as remote from
me as were those of my region, in the days of my splen-
dour" (*M* 108/66); why, in that of Malone, "my feet are
leagues away, and to call them in . . . would I think take
me over a month, exclusive of the time required to locate
them" (*MM* 99/234); why, for the Unnamable, in its incip-
ient incarnation as Worm, for instance, "this feeling of being entirely enclosed, and yet nothing touching me, is new
. . . I don't know where I end" (*I* 97/345); or why, especially in *The Unnamable*, the narrator finds itself at times
within, at times without a head, at times, indeed, between
inside and outside, as a "pure ear" (*I* 112/354) or a "tym-

panum" (*I* 160/383). Nor does this failure simply account, in its specifically auditory and visual dimensions, for the spatiality of the text itself, as the written transposition of a voice whose amplification, relative to the subject's capacity to "restrict" it, appears in the loss of the paragraph (of which there are, in the original, but two, the second covering 143 pages), if not yet the sentence, in the first part of *Molloy*, in the fragmentation of both in *Malone Dies*, and in *The Unnamable*, after an initial effort to articulate, in the loss of the paragraph (of which the last, in the original, covers 184 pages) and the virtual abandonment of the sentence as well—all of which, to be sure, can make the reading of the trilogy, like the movement of its characters and/ or narrators, an incessant coming and going "in the depths of an instant without bounds, where the light never changes and the wrecks look all alike" (*MM* 97/233), or else "a veritable calvary, with no limit to its stations and no hope of crucifixion" (*M* 129/78). Rather, as I have just suggested, this sensory dispossession, transforming perception itself, as a means of representation and in particular of spatial separation, into its own "object," contributes by analogy to the understanding of why, in the essentially verbal universe of the trilogy, an ever greater emphasis is placed on its one and only means of representation, that is, language or signification. In fact, it would be more accurate here to repeat that, in the Beckettian *oeuvre*, the failure of the senses, by virtue of which the body is reinscribed as an intersubjective "impropriété" that both produces and expropriates the "corps propre," figures the dispossession of sense itself, whereby, in its reappearance, the body of the sign is reinscribed as an intersubjective non-self-coincidence that both invests and exceeds its disappearance in the Husserlian "solitary mental life." Now that we have moved from the representation of failure to the failure of representation, it becomes clear that the compulsion and the impossibility associated at once with the movement and with the rest of the trilogy's characters must, as indeed we observed in the previous chapter, be attributed to the speech and the silence of its narrators. These latter suffer the obligation to speak and the inability not to do so, just as they are subject to the obligation and the inability to remain silent, insofar as each is born of the confusion of silence and speech, of an intersubjective noise against which each can shield itself only by imposing silence through speech. The expression of Beckettian intersubjectivity will accordingly resemble what was earlier called a mobile paralysis or paralyzed mobility, since its every progress regresses to the confusion of intersubjectivity itself. And yet, precisely in keeping with the univocal relation between intersubjectivity and its subjective incorporations or embodiments, the dispossessive movement of the trilogy is irreversible and hence leads, from Malone's "this exercise-book is my life" (*MM* 168/274) through the Unnamable's "ce qui se passe, ce sont des mots" (*I* 98/345)[18] or "I'm in words, made of words . . . I'm all these words" (*I* 166/386), toward the point at which, like the terminus of "one of those immutable relations between harmoniously perishing terms" (*MM* 90/229), the "je suis" and the "il est" coincide, but whose vanishing character testifies that beyond this "reduction" subsists the intersubjective "between" or "nowhere" that impels it, in Blanchot's phrase, "the ineliminable residue of being" (*EL* 342), what Beckett himself has described as "a stain upon the silence," in short, Beckett's own *corpus*. It is not surprising that this *corpus*, which, owing to its intersubjective logic, is of course not Beckett's "own," here recalls from yet another perspective the crux or the crisis of phenomenology, since it shows that subjectivity in no way more thoroughly misreads itself than as a purely spiritual voice "avant la lettre," is never more confused and benighted than when it assumes the clear distinction between a *geistige Leiblichkeit* and an inanimate *Körper*, and nowhere errs further from itself or goes further out of its way than where it thinks itself as an integral interiority or separation. It is not surprising either

---

[18] The sentence is omitted from the English translation.

that Beckett now leads us back to a context shared by Bataille and Freud, as well as Lévinas, inasmuch as his understanding of the intersubjective nature of dis-course bears a
close affinity to the interpretation of transgression in Bataille and evokes, as do many of Freud's and Lévinas's writings, a moral error involving no one.

. . .

Toward the end of his *débâcle*, Moran considers asking
Youdi's forgiveness, only to wonder: "Forgiveness for
what?" (*M* 279/168). And at the beginning of the novel,
where he senses the approach of his death, Molloy notes,
as it were in an anticipatory echo of Moran's perplexity:
"Then you try to pay attention, to consider with attention
all those dim things, saying to yourself, laboriously, It's my
fault. Fault? That was the word. But what fault?" (*M* 9/8).
It has been pointed out that Moran's mission remains irreducible to the simple apprehension of Molloy and that
its failure derives from the indeterminability of its *telos*. If,
as we may assume, it is for this failure that Moran would
ask forgiveness, and if, furthermore, this *telos* is to be understood as an intersubjective relation rather than another
person, then the indeterminability implied by the question: "Forgiveness for what?" would clearly have to do with
this relation, which, as we have seen, is also the *archē* of
Moran's quest. In Molloy's case as well, we have learned
that his quest, impelled by imperatives that "nearly all bore
on the same question, that of my relations with my
mother" (*M* 143/86), is not endowed with a purpose on the
order of another person, and that whenever Molloy so
misunderstands the *pourquoi* of his search, the imperatives
themselves leave him in the dark: "Yes, these imperatives
were quite explicit and even detailed until, having set me
in motion at last, they began to falter, then went silent,
leaving me there like a fool who neither knows where he is
going nor why he is going there" (*M* 143/86–87). But indeed, as he also remarks, these imperatives bear on the

quest(ion) of an intersubjective relation; and enough has already been said concerning this question to make of the following passage, now reread in a slightly different light, a guide to the indeterminable nature of Molloy's "fault":

> And of myself, all my life, I think I had been going to my mother, with the purpose of establishing our relations on a less precarious footing. And when I was with her, and I often succeeded, I left her without having done anything. And when I was no longer with her I was again on my way to her, hoping to do better the next time. And when I appeared to give up and to busy myself with something else, or with nothing at all any more, in reality I was hatching my plans and seeking the way to her house. (*M* 144–45/87)

The effect of Molloy's failure to accomplish "the purpose of establishing our relations on a less precarious footing" is evidently to perpetuate that very failure—which is to say that the quest(ion) itself pertains to an economy in which cause and effect are inextricably confused, and of which accomplishment or closure is not a predicate. The relation between "failure" and "fault," terms that have a common etymology, is underscored when Molloy considers remaining in the forest rather than seeking his mother:

> But I could not, stay in the forest I mean, I was not free to. That is to say I could have, physically nothing could have been easier, but I was not purely physical, I lacked something, and I would have had the feeling, if I had stayed in the forest, of going against an imperative, at least I had that impression. (*M* 142/86)

"The painful impression of committing a fault, almost a sin" (*M* 142/86) is ostensibly avoided only because of a *défaut* or lack rendered explicit by the translation of "je n'étais pas tout à fait qu'un physique" as "I was not purely physical, I lacked something." But if this lack prevents the transgression constituted by Molloy's remaining in the forest, it is clear that the inevitable failure toward which it propels him is itself no less a transgression or "fault." The

(para)logic according to which Molloy is at once unable not
to seek and unable to find, according to which the exigency that sends him on his way is also his compulsion to
lose it, implies that the description of moral error or discourse in the trilogy should abide by this recommendation
of the Unnamable's: "Set aside once and for all, at the
same time as the analogy with orthodox damnation, all
idea of beginning and end" (*I* 172/390). In other words,
even though, especially in *Molloy*, Beckett resorts to the
metaphor of the Fall, the postlapsarian mood of the trilogy
is not to be imputed to a fall *from* . . . , since, as Moran's
experience demonstrates most incontrovertibly, the paradisiacal repose of the subject is a belated illusion grounded
in the oblivion of its intersubjective non-self-coincidence.
This non-self-coincidence is both a *défaut* or lack, insofar
as it designates the incompletion or the other of closure,
and a *faute*, to the extent that this same other denotes the
intersubjective transgression of or excess over subjectivity
as closure. In economic terms, the production of closure
by an intersubjective investment that exceeds it describes
the subject as originarily a deficit, a debt or obligation of
which it is compelled to acquit itself through its own expenditure or loss. Not only does this intersubjectivity or
pour l'autre therefore involve a confusion of the fault and
its penalty, of crime and punishment; it also underlies a
paradox to which Freud often draws attention, namely,
that of a general guilt prior to any specific transgression—
or, in a Lévinasian perspective, the paradox of a responsibility that precedes the advent and exceeds the exercise of
freedom. For Lévinas, indeed, the ethical relation (*l'éthi-
que*) is essentially an intersubjective nonreciprocity or univocity that makes of subjectivity a nonindifferent difference or *pour l'autre* before it is ever a *pour-soi*, that inclines
the subject toward *autrui* while endowing it with a responsibility irreducible to any subsequent power or freedom of
assumption.[19] That the other, in Lévinas as well as in Beck-

---

[19] Moreover, as I note below, by virtue of this univocity, the very effort

ett, is fundamentally *not* another subject or person, constitutes its very alterity, no less than the very nonreciprocity
of a relation in which I am responsible for an other in no
way responsible for me, in which I must expiate a fault not
my own, in which I must suffer in the other's stead precisely because no one can take my place. In assuming the
indeterminable fault to be their own, Molloy and Moran
not only testify that there is in fact no one else—no other
person—to whom it may be imputed; they also ascribe an
essential impersonality to the transgression or moral error
of which they themselves are born. The ethical imperative
of the trilogy ("You must go on" [*I* 213/414]) does not posit
as its "finality" a *concept* of subjectivity, that is, a universality in whose economy the sacrifice of one subject for another would accrue to the indifferent identity of which
each is but a particular incarnation. Rather, the univocity
of the ethical relation defines such expenditure as a pure
gift, as a *perte sans profit*, an investment on which there is
no return and whose very irrecuperability constitutes the
irreplaceability or unicity of the individual subject. This
proximity of Beckett not only to Lévinas but also to Freud
and Bataille would thus further suggest that the question
of moral error in the trilogy is ultimately a question of life
and death. Indeed, it is in the context of deliberations relative to his own death that Molloy, who states at the outset
that "what I'd like now is to speak of the things that are
left, say my goodbyes, finish dying" (*M* 7/7), will candidly
observe: "But it is forbidden to give up and even to stop
an instant" (*M* 134–35/81). In this respect, however, *Molloy*
sooner sets the stage for *Malone Dies*, where the question

---

to assume responsibility *increases* the responsibility to be assumed—just as,
in Bataille, expenditure or transgression increases in accordance with the
effort to contain or restrict it, and as, in Beckett, the increasingly compulsive attempt to impose silence becomes, itself, ever noisier. For exem-
plary formulations of this dissymmetry in Lévinas, see *Totalité et infini*
(The Hague: Nijhoff, 1961), 74, and *Autrement qu'être ou au-delà de l'essence*
(The Hague: Nijhoff, 1974), 14.

of error in its moral dimension is first explicitly developed in terms of life and death.

The involvement of these terms is attested not only by the title and the tenor of the novel but also, to cite only one example, by the formulation of Malone's most fundamental desire, namely, "n'avoir plus jamais à mourir, d'entre les *mourants* [never have to die any more, from among the *living*]" (*MM* 151/264, my emphasis). And the association of both, or of their confusion, with moral error is stressed by a statement that posits the virtual identity or synonymity of living or dying and being guilty: "So long as it is what is called a living being you can't go wrong, you have the guilty one" (*MM* 142/259). This involvement of life and death, of sin and atonement, of cause and effect, is possible only in an economy in which the principle of identity itself, born of subjectivity as separation or discontinuity, does not obtain. Here again, the word "economy" is not used arbitrarily: the question of moral error is raised by a suffering or pain—in Lévinas's terminology, a "dolence"—correlative to an intersubjective investment that exceeds the capacity of its subjective embodiment to contain or restrict it; and while this investment yields a discontinuous or separate subject from whose misleading perspective such pain must have an identifiable reason or cause, in its excess it dispossesses the very ability to identify, to represent, in a word, to think this cause. The reason or *logos* of (inter)subjectivity as suffering or *pathos* thus approaches *itself* to the precise extent that thought, moved to think the pain by which it is engendered, attends to its own passion or failure. So does Macmann, a fallen (literally), prone likeness of Christ, turn in thought to his affliction:

> The idea of punishment came to his mind, addicted it is true to that chimera and probably impressed by the posture of the body and the fingers clenched as though in torment. And without knowing exactly what his sin was he felt full well that living was not a sufficient atonement for it or that this atonement was in itself a sin, calling for more atone-

ment, and so on, as if there could be anything but life, for the living. And no doubt he would have wondered if it was really necessary to be guilty in order to be punished but for the memory, more and more galling, of his having consented to live in his mother, then to leave her. And this again he could not see as his true sin, but as yet another atonement which had miscarried and, far from cleansing him of his sin, plunged him in it deeper than before. And truth to tell the ideas of guilt and punishment were confused together in his mind, as those of cause and effect so often are in the minds of those who continue to think. (*MM* 109/239–40)

Just as what Bataille terms "la mise à l'envers de la pensée" recalls, "in the minds of those who continue to think," an intersubjective confusion of whose projection and representation the *cogito* is but a belated effect, misconstrued as the cause of its own cause, and its Maker the effect of that effect, misinterpreted as the cause of the *cogito* itself, so here does this reversal, which, as Bataille remarks, is "la mise à l'envers de la pensée—et de la morale,"[20] return Macmann, abandoned as he already is by the Father, to a confusion of crime or guilt and punishment, of sin and atonement, beyond which a certain notion of "humanity" does not survive. For indeed, the passage demonstrates that the atonement ("peine") through which humanity would anew be "at one" with itself not only renews but also *augments* the (sense of) sin by which it is prompted. In other words, the imperative assumption of responsibility proves to be "impossible" in the precise sense that responsibility itself univocally invests and exceeds the very effort to establish its correlation or adequation to power and freedom. That life is equated with responsibility as excess or expenditure, as a *don de soi* or "damnation" (from *damnum*, loss) pure and simple, means that, here as in Bataille, it is conceived as a pure prodigality or generosity whose subjective differentiation creates a debt repayable only through the loss of the subject's life, and that this loss is, in

[20] *La Part maudite*, 64.

the Lévinasian sense of the term, "justice" itself—a justice that, however, the *pour-soi* inevitably misconstrues as unjust or inequitable, given the fundamental inadequation or lack of *justesse* between the *pour-soi* itself and the intersubjective economy that conditions it.[21] Lest these comments appear to convey a properly existentialist *ēthos*, it bears repeating that, unlike Sartre, Beckett does not describe, beyond the demise of God, the survival of a human being responsible to the extent that it is free, who is, so to speak, free to be responsible, whose obligation toward others remains grounded in the power of its separation and whose very self-expenditure never exceeds the economy of the same. The difference between the Sartrian *pour-soi* and the Beckettian *pour l'autre*, between a subject that posits itself as its own end only because it already presupposes its self, and an intersubjectivity whose only being is the dispossession of this teleology, remains irreducible.

We cannot close this section nor open the last without observing how, in *The Unnamable*, the question of moral error or dis-course is explicitly reformulated in terms of discourse or language, and as such eventually poses the question of dis-course or error in its epistemological dimension. Already in *Molloy*, speech (or writing) is portrayed as an atonement or punishment, as a *pensum* imposed due to the failure(s) whose indeterminability we have discussed and as whose repetition the task of the narrator, endowed with a *telos* as indeterminable as that of Moran's or Molloy's quest, is bound to be no less a failure. The Unnamable defines its predicament in the following way: "I have to speak, whatever that means. Having nothing to say, no words but the words of others, I have to speak" (*I* 46/314)[22]—recalling Beckett's characterization of the situation of the artist, for whom "there is nothing to express, nothing with which to express, nothing from

---

[21] On the meaning of "justice" in Lévinas, see, for example, *Autrement qu'être ou au-delà de l'essence*, 200–207.

[22] The English translation omits the next sentence in the French original: "Ne sachant pas parler, ne voulant pas parler, j'ai à parler."

which to express, no power to express, no desire to express, together with the obligation to express" (*TD* 17). The resemblance of this pensum to the failure for which it is to atone, a resemblance by virtue of which, in *The Unnamable* as in *Molloy*, crime and punishment are confused, explains why, says the Unnamable, "I confused pensum with lesson" (*I* 39/310), its lesson being no more nor less than the impossible representation of its original sin. In the case of the Unnamable more clearly than in that of its predecessors, this sin is a "long sin against the silence" (*I* 148/376) responsibility for which is born by "this voice that . . . can only be mine, since there is no one but me," but that "is not mine" (*I* 34/307), since it is precisely the voice of silence that gives voice to the self. As an expenditure born of expenditure itself, this self may be considered the legitimate child of prodigality; as an ex-pression or expiration whose expiation of "this long sin against the silence" only renews the sin itself, it may be considered the subject of that calvary "with no limit to its stations and no hope of crucifixion." In both cases, the effort to keep silent, to keep silence, what one might call *l'interdit lié à la parole*, is conditioned by its own transgression, and in the pursuit of its end succeeds therefore only in drawing attention to the failure of its means. As we have seen, this failure of language as a means or tool, disclosing a materiality Bataille defines as "the *nonlogical difference* that represents in relation to the *economy* of the universe what *crime* represents in relation to the law,"[23] characterizes literature itself as the language whose preeminent "propriété" is the dispossession of utility. Bataille, Beckett, and Lévinas all attest that signification is a *don* or gift, an unproductive expenditure, before it is ever an instrument of comprehension. From the point of view of the restricted economy, the irreducibility of language to comprehension appears suspect at best, and at worst nonsensical or aberrant. From the perspective of the general economy, however, it is this irre-

[23] "La Notion de dépense," 44; "The Notion of Expenditure," 129.

ducibility alone that makes possible the ethical relation or
pour l'autre and gives sense or meaning to subjectivity as a
nonindifferent difference whose responsibility precedes
and exceeds the understanding.

． ． ．

The ignorance professed by Moran and Molloy, by Malone
and the Unnamable or their respective delegates concerning the nature of transgression and the identity of the
transgressor is of a piece with the indeterminability of
both: as the differentiation of intersubjective excess, subjectivity is not the term of a relation but the transgression
of that separation on which knowledge itself is founded. It
is to the common genesis of epistemological and moral error that Descartes calls attention when, in the *Méditations*,
he speaks of the irreducibility of the will to understanding,
because of which "[the will] easily falls into error and sin,
and chooses the evil for the good, or the false for the
true."[24] This distraction (*égarement*), in which the subject is
deceived by appearances and mistakes the false for the
true, is clearly fostered by a force that surpasses the (limits
of the) understanding, but does so in the precise sense that
it undoes the distance implied by the perennial perceptive
metaphor of knowledge, that is, the metaphor of vision.
What this means, however, is that error in its epistemological dimension is not merely the other *of* truth, is not a
pure blindness but—and the difference is crucial—a failure of vision, a dispossession of the phenomenal interval
in which being manifests itself to subjectivity, what Blanchot calls "fascination." As the reading of Descartes no less
than of Husserl further indicates, it is philosophically necessary to "reduce" this error only because it precedes,
founds, and conditions the pursuit of truth—which is to

---

[24] *Oeuvres philosophiques*, 2:463; *Philosophical Works*, 1:176. The French
reads: "[la volonté] s'égare fort aisément, et choisit le mal pour le bien,
ou le faux pour le vrai. Ce qui fait que je me trompe et que je pèche."

say that when, as in literature, truth fails and being *as man-ifestation* dis-appears, there appears in its stead what dis-simulates itself in the phenomenality of being and its truth, "no longer dissimulated being," observes Blanchot, "but being *as* dissimulated: dissimulation itself" (*EL* 339):

> "Everything has disappeared" appears. What one calls *ap-pearance* [*apparition*] is this very fact—the "everything has dis-appeared" become in its turn appearance. And *appearance* means precisely that when everything has disappeared, there is still something: when everything is lacking, the lack brings forth [fait apparaître] the essence of being which is still to be there where it is lacking, to be as dissimulated. . . (*EL* 340)

To subjectivity as fascination thus corresponds being as dissimulation; and the space between them is not the phe-nomenal distance of separation but the space of a "*contact à distance*," a "nowhere," what Lévinas will call, among other things, *proximité*. And as the first section of this chap-ter pointed out, the "return" of this space attests to the or-igin of the distinction between "ideal" and "real" percep-tion in the imaginary dispossession of the distinction itself. Insofar as it appears to confirm such an illusory separa-tion, it is hardly sufficient therefore simply to say that vi-sion is a metaphor of knowledge; rather, the necessity of the metaphor testifies that the purported "propriété" of conceptual knowledge relies on the dissimulated "impro-priété" intrinsic to that third term of which it may be said that Descartes expressed his greatest distrust, to wit, the imagination, and that the light of knowledge is originarily "a dark light" (*MM* 106/238), "the light she had been told about," as Malone notes in reference to the desperate Mme Louis, "and told she could never understand, because it was not like those she knew [cette lumière dont on lui avait toujours dit qu'elle ne saurait la concevoir, car elle n'en était pas une à proprement parler]" (*MM* 70/216–17).

These comments certainly help to explain, within the es-sentially imaginary universe of the trilogy (whose charac-ters and/or narrators, ever more involved not only in moral error but in error generally, evolve toward "the all-impotent, all-nescient" [*I* 100/346] that is Worm), the increasing predominance of greyness. Molloy himself is grey (*M* 13/10) and moves under "a pale and dying sky" (*M* 106/65). Malone lives in a room where "it is never light . . . never really light" but that bathes in a kind of "grey incandescence," "in a kind of leaden light that makes no shadow, so that it is hard to say from what direction it comes, for it seems to come from all directions at once, and with equal force" (*MM* 76/220–21),[25] and observes of himself: "I myself am very grey, I even sometimes have the feeling that I emit grey" (*MM* 77/221). And the Unnamable, deprived even of the "outside" against which Malone can attempt to measure the leaden light of his room, states of the air surrounding it that "close to me it is grey, dimly transparent, and beyond that charmed circle deepens and spreads its fine impenetrable veils," wondering, "Is it I who cast the faint light that enables me to see what goes on under my nose?" (*I* 22/300), and later characterizing its medium as "the changeless round of imperfect shadow and dubious light" (*I* 35/307), even as a "grey silence" (*I* 131/365). But indeed, the question immediately arises as to the relation between this grey and this silence, between a "color" in which black and white are confused and a "sound" that is neither speech nor silence, between the medium of a visual dispossession and its auditory or acoustic analogue, or more simply between the eye and the ear. This question is indirectly raised by Descartes himself when he concludes that "this proposition: *I am, I exist,* is necessarily true each

[25] In the trilogy, greyness is associated not only with spatial but also with temporal uncertainty. Perhaps the most striking example is offered by Malone, who, having one night awaited the light of dawn, confides: "But the light, instead of being the dawn, turned out in a very short time to be the dusk. And the sun, instead of rising higher and higher in the sky as I confidently expected, calmly set, and night, the passing of which I had just celebrated after my fashion, calmly fell again" (*MM* 75–76/220).

time that I pronounce it, or that I mentally conceive it."[26] Be it "conceived" or, more pointedly, "pronounced," the proposition *I am*, or rather the truth of that proposition, depends entirely on its repetition. As we have seen, this repetition necessarily describes the time (here: "fois") of the *I am* as a *différance*, and hence necessarily describes the identity of the *I* as the reappearance or re-semblance of this difference, its *logos* as, so to speak, an *ana-logos*, and the truth of the proposition *I am* as at best a *vraie semblance*. In the terms of Derrida's critique of Husserl, or those of the trilogy itself, the voice that pronounces "I am" is analogous to a writing to the extent that, as writing supplements speech, so speech supplements a subject that is already, by virtue of its non-self-identity, "structured like a language," like signification, like writing. The question of the relation between the eye and the ear, between the grey(ness) and the noise of the trilogy, can therefore be answered only if, in their substantial distinction, the two terms are understood to designate one and the same functional difference: just as the speaking subject is unable to impose the silence that is its proper sense save by reproducing the auditory contamination that conditions it, so the writing subject cannot make sense of this "impropriété" otherwise than through an inscription whose own sense remains forever between the twin alternatives enunciated by Molloy when he insists that "you would do better, at least no worse, to obliterate texts than to blacken margins" (*M* 18/13). In short, the "grey silence" of the trilogy refers to an intersubjective *écart* that is both the possibility of (proper) sense, insofar as it entails a repetition yielding the sameness *of* the *écart* itself, and its impossibility, to the extent that this sameness is but the re-semblance of a non-self-identity that, in itself, "has" no sense—and so also and at once the possibility and the impossibility of truth or of knowledge, whether these be understood as adequation or

---

[26] *Oeuvres philosophiques*, 2:415–16; *Philosophical Works*, 1:150.

as what is variously called *alētheia*, manifestation, phenomenality, separation.

Perhaps nowhere in the trilogy is the (un)grounding of
truth in an error that precedes and conditions the very distinction between truth and falsehood more clearly defined,
especially in relation to the telling of stories, than in the
case of Moran, who notes concerning his pensum, that is,
his storytelling:

> For it is one of the features of this penance that I may not
> pass over what is over and straightway come to the heart of
> the matter. But that must again be unknown to me which is
> no longer so and that again fondly believed which then I
> fondly believed, at my setting out. (*M* 221/133)

This passage, already quoted in another context, defines
the truth of whose knowledge Moran is only belatedly possessed as the repetition of his earlier ignorance or error.
And since this error is an *écart* that dispossesses the very
foundation of knowledge, the knowledge *of* this error
must be stated negatively ("It was not midnight. It was not
raining"), as the knowledge of a *non-savoir*. Moreover, the
undecidable ambiguity or equivocity evoked by these concluding lines defines an intersubjective *écart* whose univocal relation to the subject(s) it produces not only accounts,
as we have observed, for the *fêlure* of Moran's story, or
rather for Moran himself *as fêlure* and for his compulsion
to (re)tell the impossible story of his failure, but also explains why the *écart* itself is reproduced, with ever greater
impoverishment, in the trilogy's subsequent narrators.
The lack or excess constitutive of Molloy's quest, corresponding in moral terms to its sin(fulness) or atonement,
corresponds epistemologically to the unavoidable inadequation of his discourse, so that he is able to tell the truth
of intersubjectivity only as it were "à son insu," that is, only
by failing to tell truth as adequation:

> For I always say either too much or too little, which is a ter-
> rible thing for a man with a passion for truth like mine. . . .

It often happened to me, before I gave up speaking for
good, to think I had said too little when in fact I had said too
much and in fact to have said too little when I thought I had
said too much. I mean that on reflexion, in the long run
rather, my verbal profusion turned out to be penury, and
inversely. So time sometimes turns the tables. In other
words, or perhaps another thing, whatever I said it was
never enough and always too much. (*M* 53–54/34)

It is this confusion of the "too much" and the "too little,"
of "profusion" and "penury," that fosters, as for Moran, an
ignorance (or belief) of which the only knowledge to be
obtained amounts to its own demystification, and which,
since it remains the latter's condition, describes the *epistēmē*
of Beckettian intersubjectivity as the endless ironization of
its subjects' *doxa*. In the case of Malone, of course, the same
mystifying *écart* is articulated somewhat differently, coinciding with the space between a third-person narrative
wherein Malone portrays himself as another and a first-
person (meta)narrative in which he portrays himself as the
same. The resulting ambiguity, whereby it is impossible to
decide which of the narratives is excessive and which in-
sufficient, characterizes the narrator as the being of their
écart, whose inevitable corollary is formulated by Malone
himself when he remarks that "I shall go on doing as I
have always done, not knowing what it is I do, nor who I
am, nor where I am, nor if I am" (*MM* 85/226). Malone
thus anticipates the "end" of the trilogy, and also points to
a certain anti-intellectualist tendency of Beckett's thought,
by locating the invisible horizon of the Beckettian universe
beyond separation and the reified understanding to which
it gives rise.

The last of those many forms "in which the unchanging
seeks relief from its formlessness" (*MM* 38/197), namely,
the Unnamable, whose name already states its own inadequation, labors to the end and beyond within an aporia of
which it says, at the beginning, that "I say aporia without
knowing what it means" (*I* 8/291), pursuing in vain its re-

pose in the very unthinkable unspeakable "space between" where there can be none:

> It's a lot to expect of one creature, it's a lot to ask, that he should first behave as if he were not, then as if he were, before being admitted to that peace where he neither is, nor is not, and where the language dies that permits of such expressions. Two falsehoods, two trappings, to be borne to the end, before I can be let loose, alone, in the unthinkable unspeakable, where I have not ceased to be, where they will not let me be. (*I* 80/334–35)

As the previous chapter pointed out, the "they" of *The Unnamable* designates the indeterminable intersubjectivity of discourse itself, which its subjective differentiation is at once compelled and unable to reveal by means of a language whose terms have always already been dispossessed. The univocity of this dispossession posits its terminus as the impossible coincidence of the subject or sign and its self, where the long history of error would yield an apocalyptic truth in no need of words. Failing this, the Beckettian subject is condemned to ex-press itself, to live "cette perpétuelle erreur, qui est précisément la 'vie,' " to tell the truth of that creature who will never know what Proust calls the happiness of those "for whom, near though the one may be to the other, the hour of truth has struck before the hour of death."[27]

[27] Marcel Proust, *A la recherche du temps perdu*, ed. Pierre Clarac and André Ferré (Paris: Gallimard, Bibliothèque de la Pléiade, 1954), 3:910; *Remembrance of Things Past*, trans. C. Scott Moncrieff, Terence Kilmartin, and Andreas Mayor (New York: Random House, 1981), 3:948.

THE ENDS OF LITERATURE

The present study has attempted to show how Samuel Beckett defines the "subject of literature" in terms of a general economy of signification that conditions and exceeds the universe of phenomenology. By problematizing what is both the *archē* and the *telos* of this universe, namely, separation, Beckett's work—and most notably his trilogy of novels—raises even today the very questions most intensely debated at the time of the trilogy's composition. I refer of course to the question of the ends of literature as well as to the more general but closely related question of the ends of humanity. That we are just beginning to hear Beckett's voice indicates how thoroughly this debate was dominated by an ideology to which his own point of view remains radically irreducible. The purpose of this brief conclusion is to describe, specifically in reference to the problem of such "ends," the difference between Beckett's perspective and the existential humanism that prevailed in postwar France.

As I noted in both the preface and the introduction, existential humanism derived from a phenomenological understanding of subjectivity. In postwar France, perhaps more generally in postwar Europe, the most celebrated proponent of phenomenology and its ideological derivative was Jean-Paul Sartre, whose own best-known statement concerning literature and the human subject undoubtedly remains the lengthy text entitled *Qu'est-ce que la littérature?*, first published in 1947.

The indebtedness of Sartre's theory of literature to phenomenology is clear from the very first pages of this treatise. In fact, although mention is nowhere made of Husserl, the resemblance of the Sartrian distinction between

prose and poetry to the Husserlian distinction between expression and indication is quite palpable. Just as, for Husserl, the expressive signifier is possessed of a pure transparency distinguished from the opacity of its indicative
contrary, so, for Sartre, "there is prose when the word
passes across our gaze as the glass across the sun,"[1] that is,
when the visibility intrinsic to the poetic signifier itself has
been reduced. Moreover, both Sartre and Husserl recognize the ideality of these originary distinctions; both avow
that, in reality, they do not obtain.[2] And finally, in Sartre
no less than in Husserl, the acknowledgment of this theoretical fiction suggests that the point of departure is a
purely normative *telos* in disguise. In other words, what is
presented as a given property of language turns out to be
an *exigency*, one whose "impossibility" is attested, as we
have seen, by the aporetic character of distinction or separation itself, which can be realized only if it forsakes the
ideality on which its very existence depends. To be sure,
Husserl's concerns in the *Logische Untersuchungen* are primarily epistemological, whereas those of Sartre in *Qu'est-ce*

---

[1] Jean-Paul Sartre, *Qu'est-ce que la littérature?* (Paris: Gallimard, 1948;
Gallimard, Idées, 1972), 27; *What is Literature?*, trans. Bernard Frechtman
(London: Methuen, 1950), 11. All further references to this work (henceforth *QL*) will be given in the text and will include the page number of
the French original, followed, after a slash, by the page number of
the English translation, which has occasionally been modified. The first
version of *Qu'est-ce que la littérature?* was published in *Les Temps modernes*
17–22 (February–July 1947). The definitive version then appeared in *Situations 2* (Paris: Gallimard, 1948).

[2] For Husserl, see, for example, *Logische Untersuchungen*, vol. 2, pt. 1,
90–91 (*Logical Investigations*, 1:321–22), and the introduction to this
study. For Sartre, see n. 5, *QL* 48/25. In this note, where reference is also
made to a notion of failure one might instructively contrast with Beckett's
own, Sartre concedes that "it is for the purpose of greater clarity that I
have considered the extreme cases of pure prose and pure poetry," and
concludes: "It is a question of complex and impure but well-delimited
structures." However, he cannot have it both ways: for if, *in fact*, both
prose and poetry are impure, then their real "delimitation" remains irreducible to the ideal distinction upon which the very "clarity" or intelli-
gibility of his position is predicated.

que la littérature? are largely ethico-political. Yet the analogy holds regardless of this difference and clearly implies that Sartre could be no more successful in "committing" literature than was Husserl in eliminating the indicative contamination of expression. It remains to be seen precisely why this is so and what are the consequences of such a failure.

What Sartre proposes is a "cleansing" ("nettoyage") or "curing" ("guérison") of language.[3] The sickness or impurity targeted by this operation is none other than the ambiguity that, according to Sartre, determines two possible attitudes toward the linguistic sign: "The ambiguity of the sign implies that one can penetrate it at will like a pane of glass and pursue the thing signified, or turn one's gaze toward its *reality* and consider it as an object" (*QL* 18/5). Instead of examining this ambiguity as it pertains to the sign *in general*, Sartre, like Husserl, insists on distinguishing between what he considers to be two radically heterogeneous types of sign, or again, between two incompatible attitudes toward language, either of which can apparently be adopted at will: the prosaic, which "reduces," negates, or effaces the sign in order to grasp its referent, and the poetic, which focuses on the sign itself. However, no sooner has Sartre posited this distinction, recognizably corresponding to the ontological polarity of nothingness and being, than he is led to modify it. The poetic word, it turns out, is not a mere thing or object, but continues to signif albeit in a manner not to be confused with that of pr and which Sartre describes as follows:

> [The word's] sonority, its length, its masculine or femin
> endings, its visual aspect, compose for it a face of flesh
> *represents* rather than expresses meaning. Inversely, a
> meaning is *realized*, the physical aspect of the word
> flected within it, and it, in its turn, functions as an im

---

[3] "If we want to restore their virtue to words, we must car analytical cleansing [nettoyage] which rids them of their meanings" (*QL* 342/211); "If words are sick, it is up to us to them" (*QL* 341/210).

[3] "If we want to restore their virtue to words, we must carry out . . . an analytical cleansing [nettoyage] which rids them of their adventitious meanings" (*QL* 342/211); "If words are sick, it is up to us to cure [guérir] them" (*QL* 341/210).

the verbal body. As its sign, too, for it has lost its pre-eminence; since words, like things, are given, the poet does not
decide whether the former exist for the latter or vice versa.

Thus, between the word and the thing signified, there is
established a double reciprocal relation of magical resemblance and meaning. And since the poet does not *utilize* the
word, he does not choose between different senses given to
it; each of them, instead of appearing to him as an autono-
mous function, is given to him as a material quality that
merges before his eyes with the other accepted meanings.
(*QL* 20–21/6–7)

According to Sartre, then, what distinguishes the poetic
word is that its *body*—"its sonority, its length, its masculine
or feminine endings, its visual aspect," in short, its "face of
flesh"—is capable of meaning or signifying. All that which,
due to its materiality, due to its social and historical contingency, is for the Sartrian model of the prose writer the
mere dross of authorial intention, remains absolutely essential to poetic language. This characterization of the poetic sign as *both* body and mind, object and subject, already
suggests that the "curing" or "cleansing" mentioned above
will consist of relegating the ambiguity of the sign in general to poetry alone. But that is not all. For the ambiguity
of the poetic attitude is contagious: not only does it ascribe
to the body of the sign a function normally reserved for its
spiritual effacement, but this very incorporation or "realization" of meaning transforms the thing signified into an
"image" or "sign" of its own sign. As a result, the separation of "words" and "things" and the hierarchy it implies—
the "pre-eminence" of things—are called into question.
"Poetry" designates not the other of prose but an alterity
irreducible to their distinction and whose equivocity or
ambiguity suspends the teleological movement of prose
signification. It is undoubtedly for this reason that Sartre
directs his severest criticism not at poetry "in itself" (that
is, in the purely ideal and, as we have just seen, invalid
sense of a pure opacity), but rather at its contamination or

infection of prose: "In many cases modern literature is a cancer of words. . . . In particular, there is nothing more deplorable [néfaste] than the literary practice which, I believe, is called poetic prose and which consists of using words for the obscure harmonics resounding about them and made up of vague meanings in contradiction with the clear meaning" (QL 341/210). Prose can only be itself if it is cleansed or cured of the vagueness and obscurity associated with poetry and more generally with an economy that does not lend itself to clarity and distinction (and whose instances include, as Sartre suggests, painting, sculpture, and music).[4] Inasmuch as poetry so understood—that is, as the other of distinction itself—corresponds to the present study's definition of literature as a dispossession of the proper, one can say that the theory of literature in *Qu'est-ce que la littérature?* envisages a "reduction" of literature itself, just as Husserl's theory of the sign purports to reduce its own *raison d'être*. The question now arises as to the nature of that "end" in whose name a pure prose, like a pure expression, is to be sought.

That pure prose itself remains *to be sought* suggests that the end in question may very well coincide, as it does in Husserl, with the effacement of signification as a means. Indeed, we have already seen how Sartre compares prose to a perfectly transparent pane of glass. He also makes quite explicit his understanding of its utilitarian character: "Prose is, in essence, utilitarian. I would readily define the prose-writer as a man who *makes use* of words" (QL 26/10). And finally, while Sartre's concerns are ultimately ethical and political, he first grants to the sign *as tool* an epistemological value: "It is in and by language conceived as a certain kind of instrument that the search for truth takes place [s'opère]" (QL 17/5). As questionable as one may find the assumption that literary prose is a search for truth, it

---

[4] In the course of distinguishing between the prosaic and the poetic "uses" of language, Sartre states that "poetry is on the side of painting, sculpture, and music" (QL 17/4).

may initially be more fruitful to ask what form of truth Sartre has in mind. The answer is, of course, quite predictable. As the analogy with Husserl would lead us to expect, what Sartre seeks is revealed truth, grounded in a phenomenological understanding of the human subject: "Each of our perceptions is accompanied by the consciousness that human reality is 'disclosive' ['dévoilante'], in other words, that through it 'there is' being, or, to put it yet another way, that man is the means by which things are manifested" (*QL* 49/26). But if humanity is a means whose end is manifestation or disclosure, it must suffer the same fate as the sign in pure prose. In other words, just as, in pure prose, the instantaneous effacement of the sign defines it as a means coinciding with manifestation as the end of literature, so manifestation or disclosure as the end of humanity requires that the definition of humanity as a means comprise a certain negation or reduction. In both cases— that of the sign, that of humanity—this negation bears on the body. Sartre must assume two radically distinct definitions of human being, or more precisely, he must assume human being to *be* a distinction or separation whose terms correspond, as indicated by his understanding of the sign, to the mind and the body, the for-itself and the in-itself. For if manifestation is indeed the end of humanity, humanity in its turn is necessarily modeled on a subject whose separation from exteriority, including its own body, makes manifestation itself possible. And here as always, separation entails hierarchy: Sartrian humanism excludes the body from the *essence* of humanity, that is, it demands that humanity, in order to achieve this essence or ideal identity, be "cured" or "cleansed" of its real ambiguity. In epistemological terms, the end in whose name a pure prose is to be sought amounts therefore to the truth of this identity or sameness, in which, separated from exteriority, subjectivity discloses the latter while manifesting itself. The prosaic "search for truth" seeks to totalize being as an economy of the same or *to auto* wherein language itself would be perfectly tauto-logical. Whence Sartre's dogmatic assertion: "The function of a writer is to call a spade a spade [La fonction d'un écrivain est d'appeler un chat un chat]" (*QL* 341/210).

From this, there follows a veritable multitude of consequences, of which I would like to emphasize two. First, such a totalization—the "total renewal [reprise] of the world [at which] the creative act aims" (*QL* 72/41)—is only conceivable if the creator is granted a position absolutely analogous to that of God. Sartre begins to answer the question "Why write?" by claiming that "one of the chief motives of artistic creation is certainly the need to feel that we are essential in relation to the world" (*QL* 50/26–27). As opposed to the world in which perception discloses an object that the subject has not produced and in relation to which the subject remains therefore inessential, the world of the artist is one in which "the creation becomes inessential in relation to the creative activity" (*QL* 51/27). The artist thus realizes the essence of humanity to the extent that he or she produces his or her own separation from being and is consequently both free and able to represent being in its totality, *as* a world. The problem here is, however, immediately apparent. For this power and this freedom, as well as the separation upon which they are predicated, pertain to a purely ideal subject the assumption of whose position by any real or empirical counterpart would require nothing less than the latter's own death. The impossibility of such an assumption implies that the freedom and power, the separation of the Sartrian "subject of literature" and the world whose totality this subject purports to represent, are in reality strictly imaginary. And Sartre says as much: "For this is indeed the final goal of art: to recover this world by giving it to be seen as it is, but *as if* it had its source in human freedom" (*QL* 72–73/41, my emphasis). The crucial "as if" indicates that (real) freedom is precisely *not* the source of this world or its literature but, *in essence*, an exigency whose accomplishment necessarily remains suspended in the imaginary *écart* between the real and the ideal. The writer whose absolute separation would entail

the freedom and the power to silence the noise of intersubjectivity—the writer who would "call a spade a spade"—
turns out to be a fiction undone by the very language it
claims to use as a means to that end.

The second of the consequences mentioned above may
be considered a corollary of the first and pertains to the
relation between this writer and his or her reader(s). It is
here indeed that the ethico-political imperative informing
Sartre's theory of literature finds its clearest articulation.
For if "the work can be defined as an imaginary presentation of the world insofar as it demands human freedom"
(*QL* 79/45), and if, as Sartre further claims, the writer,
whose activity is expected to originate in freedom, in turn
requires the reader to lend to this presentation an *objective*
truth, then "the writer chooses to appeal to the freedom of
other men so that, by the reciprocal implications of their
demands, they may re-adapt the totality of being to man
and may again enclose the universe within humanity [pour
que . . . ils réapproprient la totalité de l'être à l'homme et
referment l'humanité sur l'univers]" (*QL* 73/41).[5] Thus,
the intersubjective relation is understood as a dialectical
reciprocity grounded in separation, the reader being modeled on the writer, that is, defined as a(nother) subject possessed from the outset of the very freedom and power to
whose nonoriginarity the work itself is supposed to testify.
As Blanchot has pointed out, in a response to *Qu'est-ce que
la littérature?* entitled "La littérature et le droit à la mort,"[6]
this appeal is essentially an empty one: given that, any
more than in the case of the writer, no real, living reader
can assume the absolute separation required to "re-adapt

[5] The curious prefix in "réapproprient" and "referment" rather clearly
indicates the unwarranted assumption of a prelapsarian world corresponding, as I earlier suggested, to a disguised *telos*. And this is to say
nothing of Sartre's sexist idiom: if we substitute "women" and "woman"
for "men" and "man," does the statement as a whole continue to make
sense?

[6] Maurice Blanchot, "La littérature et le droit à la mort," in *La Part du
feu* (Paris: Gallimard, 1949), especially 306–11.

the totality of being to man and . . . again [to] enclose the universe within humanity," the call to action is addressed to no one. Or, to put it another way, again following Blanchot: the call to action demands of the subject to whom it is addressed the sacrifice of its particularity in the name of human(ist) universality. In still other words—and here Blanchot alludes to Hegel as much as to Sartre—the literature of action seeks to realize ideality, that is, to make of freedom and power the power and the freedom *not* to be, to institute not only the "right to die" but death itself as the ultimate human "possibility," the end of humanity. To say that this realization would in fact entail the absence of any subject endowed with such attributes is to state the obvious. For our purposes, the point is yet again that literature, as one instance of an economy whose principle is the very failure of negation, could never serve as a means to this end.

Indeed, the reader of Beckett's trilogy would sooner conclude that literature is the very dispossession of the end, in both senses of the term. For as we have seen, the speech by means of which subjectivity would impose the silence supposedly proper to it only renews the intersubjective noise in which subjectivity itself originates, while the very necessity of this ex-pression defines the death of the subject as anything but a possibility. In other words, the end, for Beckett, is not the *telos* of a totalizing dialectic impelled by negation or separation but the failure of separation itself as a principle. Rather than as the freedom and the power not to be or to speak, the origin of the Beckettian "subject of literature" in this essentially affirmative failure describes its being as a compulsion and a powerlessness, an exigency and an impossibility, the obligation to speak and the inability not to do so. Condemned to reopen the ambiguous or imaginary *écart* between the real and the ideal, between the "je suis" and the "il est," the subject of the trilogy does not end in apocalypse but, as an *autrement qu'être*, exceeds the end itself, thereby testifying to the excess of signification in general over the phenomenological dream of totality.

If Beckett's work appears therefore to demand a general reconsideration of literature, including most notably its authorship, it is clearly not with a view toward closing the question thus opened. And if, like Lévinas, Beckett ascribes an irreplaceability to the human subject, it is certainly not, any more than Lévinas, as a *belle âme* nostalgic for another humanism, for that individuality which is but the reverse of totalitarian thought. Articulating a universe whose principle is essentially other than the distinction or separation on which humanism and its reduction of literature are founded, the Beckettian *oeuvre* transforms our understanding of both literature and humanity by transforming the very conditions of that understanding. To summarize the "lesson" of the trilogy, one could say, paraphrasing Libertson, that while literature cannot change the world, it remains nonetheless the world's alteration.

INDEX

ability. *See* power
action, 8, 48, 67
allegory, 46n.20, 56–57, 64, 67,
72–74, 101, 107, 110
"already," the, 36–39, 42–43, 50–
54, 56, 58, 60–61, 64, 69, 73
alterity. *See* difference
archē, 14, 16, 19, 21, 50, 60, 74,
95, 100, 119, 124, 144, 160. *See
also* origin
art, ix, 7, 10, 27, 29, 30, 32, 97,
130–31, 151, 166
"as though," the, 38–39, 64, 101,
110–11, 133, 135. *See also*
conditionality
atonement, 149–52
authorship, 105–8, 115, 118, 169
à venir, the, 26, 36–37, 51, 52, 69,
131

Bakhtin, M. M., 103n
Bataille, Georges, x, 5, 6n.8, 33,
75, 77–86, 91, 94, 95, 107, 118,
119, 121, 123, 145, 148, 150,
152
Beckett, Samuel, ix–x, 3–10, 27–
29, 32–33, 39–65, 66–77,
84n.16, 91, 94–122, 131–32,
135–59, 160, 168–69. Works:
"Le Calmant," 4; *Comment c'est*,
4n.5; *Eleuthéria*, 3; *Endgame*,
56n; "L'Expulsé," 4; "La Fin," 4;
Malone Dies, 3, 57n, 61–64, 66–
67, 76, 102–3, 105, 108–14,
116, 143, 148–50; *Mercier et
Camier*, 3, 4n.5; *Molloy*, 3, 34,
39–62, 64n.32, 66–74, 76, 97–
103, 105, 108–10, 119, 131–32,
135–38, 143, 145–48, 151; *Nou-*

velles et textes pour rien, 3; "Premier amour," 3, 4; *Proust*, 6;
Stirrings Still, 4n.5; *Textes pour
rien*, 3n.1, 4, 58n; "Three Dialogues," 6–7, 9–10, 33; *The Unnamable*, 3, 61–67, 76, 97, 101–
3, 105–6, 108–9, 113–18, 142–
43, 151–52, 158–59; *Waiting for
Godot*, 3, 46n.20, 56n; *Watt*,
4n.5, 46n.19, 101
being, 8–9, 30, 64, 81–82, 101,
112–13, 153–54, 162
belatedness, 22–23, 36–37, 56,
64–65, 71–72. *See also* supplementarity
Benjamin, Walter, 65, 118n.57
Blanchot, Maurice, x, 5, 8–9,
22n.20, 27, 29, 33, 66, 70, 75,
79, 84n.16, 103, 104n.35, 106–
9, 112–18, 121, 125–31, 141,
144, 153–54, 167–68
binding, 88–89, 95, 119, 139
body, 14–15, 17–18, 33, 39, 55,
93, 140–41, 143–44, 163, 165

causality, 23–24, 36, 133–34, 149–
50
Chambers, Ross, 34n
character, 56, 62n, 98–100, 107,
110, 135, 137
closure, 49, 146–47
cogito, 23–24, 30–32, 44, 127n,
134, 150
communication, 6n.8, 12, 15, 17,
35, 42, 58, 63, 75, 108–9, 118,
131
compulsion, 6n.8, 27, 62, 85, 98,
105, 114–15, 127n, 139, 140,